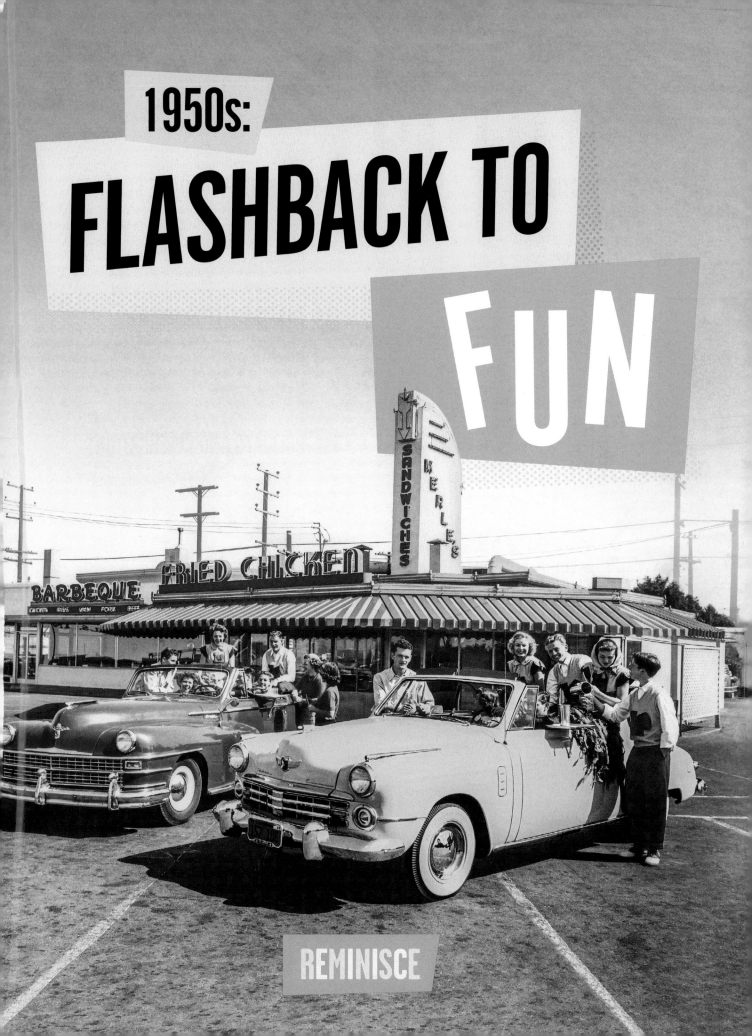

1950s:
FLASHBACK TO
FUN

SANDWICHES

MERLE'S

FRIED CHICKEN

BARBEQUE

REMINISCE

CONTENTS

PICTURED ON FRONT COVER:
Drive-in on page 74, courtesy of the California History Room, California State Library, Sacramento, California
Couple on page 66, John Douglas "Doug" Green
John Wayne on page 135, Ann Dufour
Kids sledding on page 28, Harry Jungi

PICTURED ON BACK COVER:
Easter hat on page 195, Joan Houseman
Human pyramid on page 98, Paula Hassler
Kool-Aid ad on page 30

PHOTO COLORIZATION FOR COVER AND CHAPTER OPENERS: Sanna Dullaway

© 2018 RDA Enthusiast Brands, LLC.
1610 N. 2nd St., Suite 102, Milwaukee, WI 53212-3906

International Standard Book Number: 978-1-61765-798-6
Library of Congress Control Number: 2018939398
Component Number: 117300060H

In 1950 Branchville, New Jersey, this diverse group of bicyclists used the drugstore, which was a combination general store and ice cream parlor, as a local hangout.

A Decade to Remember

The 1950s were a time full of prosperity for much of America. If you, like so many of us, are longing for those good ol' days, this delightful collection of stories is sure to warm hearts and get you reminiscing with family and friends.

1950s: Flashback to Fun is a keepsake that brings back the life and spirit of the era. Memories include tales of what it was like to be a kid growing up in this post-World War II period of consumerism, the importance of family, blossoming romance and the traditions of the time surrounding it, quirky kitchen fads, the fashions donned, and recollections of drive-in movie theaters and diners, along with the cars that got us there.

Stories reveal the men and women who were hard at work during this period and those who went off to defend our country in Korea. Plus, you'll find accounts of the iconic music that overtook a generation and the TV shows like *American Bandstand*, *I Love Lucy* and *Leave It to Beaver* that kept viewers hooked as television sets were welcomed into more and more American households.

This armchair look back will pull you in with peeks at Hollywood, sports, holiday celebrations and more during the decade.

We hope you love the collection and the more than 330 vintage photos and advertisements throughout, plus the bonus historical timeline of the '50s.

—The editors of *Reminisce* magazine

1950 TO 1959: A LOOK BACK

The fads, faces and history of the 1950s are true iconic Americana. It was a time of drive-ins, Hula-Hoops, Elvis and the rise of suburbia. Before you dive into this journey, take a moment to look back at the events that made the 1950s such a compelling and unforgettable time in U.S. history.

1950

TV's most widely watched hour is the *Texaco Star Theatre* with Milton Berle, although ***Kukla, Fran & Ollie,*** a children's puppet show, is making a mark with 6 million viewers.

Diners Club cards are rolled out as the world's first multipurpose charge card, to the delight of families everywhere.

President Harry S. Truman authorizes the use of U.S. troops to repel the North Korean invasion of South Korea, marking the beginning of the Korean War and a decade of bomb fear.

Sen. Joseph McCarthy, R-Wis., creates a stir by claiming that Communists working in the U.S. State Department are shaping the country's foreign policy.

■ Charles Schulz introduces Charlie Brown to America as the *Peanuts* comic strip debuts.

■ The first television remote controls are introduced.

Boston Red Sox star Ted Williams makes news when he signs on for the 1950 season with a record-setting $125,000 contract.

1951

After Gen. Douglas MacArthur urges an attack on positions within China itself, President Truman relieves him of his command.

One of America's first suburban malls, Shoppers World, opens in Framingham, Massachusetts.

The U.S. Census Bureau buys **UNIVAC,** the first commercially produced, large-scale business computer.

New York Yankee **Mickey Mantle** hits his first home run.

The Public Health Service reports that fluoridation of water supplies greatly reduces tooth decay.

The first direct-dial long-distance telephone call links mayors in Englewood, New Jersey, and Alameda, California.

1952

Mr. Potato Head and Les Paul's solid-body **Gibson guitar** are introduced.

Theatergoers flock to see *Bwana Devil,* the first full-length color motion picture in **3D**, and receive special glasses that bring the action up close.

At the Indianapolis 500 auto race, Troy Ruttman becomes the youngest winner ever at age 22. His average speed of 128.9 mph sets a course record.

■ Kemmons Wilson launches the first Holiday Inn hotel, in Memphis, Tennessee.

■ The first political campaign commercials air on television.

■ Dwight D. "Ike" Eisenhower and Richard M. Nixon, Republican nominees for president and vice president, win the election.

■ The U.S. ends the occupation in Japan.

After the death of King George VI, England sees the beginning of the long reign of his older daughter, **Elizabeth II.**

1953

Edmund Hillary of New Zealand and **Tenzing Norgay,** a Nepalese Sherpa tribesman, become the first men to reach the summit of Mount Everest and return.

Cambridge University scientists Francis Crick and James Watson discover the **double-helix structure of DNA,** which leads to technologies such as genetic engineering and DNA fingerprinting.

General Motors introduces the **Chevrolet Corvette.**

■ Dwight Eisenhower takes office as the first Republican president in 20 years.

■ Hugh Hefner publishes the first issue of *Playboy.*

In Korea, a truce is signed at Panmunjom, ending the fighting of the Korean War, although without a peace treaty.

■ The Supreme Court ends lunch-counter segregation in Washington, D.C.

■ Bob Hope hosts the 25th Academy Awards, the first ceremony broadcast on television.

1954

Famous fictional collie *Lassie* debuts on TV.

- Roughly 29 million U.S. households have **television sets.**

- *People Are Funny* with Art Linkletter and ***Father Knows Best*** with Robert Young debut on TV, making the transition from radio.

- Disney's *Davy Crockett* premieres and quickly becomes a national craze.

A postwar building boom continues, and the New York Stock Exchange has its most active year since 1933.

Transistor radios become widely available, although the sound is reported as "tinny."

Amid a continuing outbreak of polio, massive field trials begin to test the effectiveness of Dr. Jonas Salk's polio vaccine on children. The vaccine works.

1955

Albert Einstein, one of the greatest scientific minds of all time, dies in Princeton, New Jersey.

- The first edition of *The Guinness Book of Records* is published.

- Ford challenges the Chevrolet Corvette with the Thunderbird.

Rosa Lee Parks refuses to give up her seat, setting in motion the Montgomery bus boycott in Alabama.

The Brooklyn Dodgers win their first World Series, beating the New York Yankees. They had lost seven Series previously—five to the Yankees.

- Rising actor James Dean dies in a car accident in Cholame, California.

- English Prime Minister Sir Winston Churchill resigns.

Disneyland opens in California.

1956

Robby the Robot and some neat special effects make *The Forbidden Planet* a movie success, starring Leslie Nielsen.

The Eisenhower-Nixon ticket wins the election, marking the first time in the century that a Republican president has been elected to consecutive terms.

Boxer Rocky Marciano retires as the only undefeated heavyweight champion in boxing history.

■ The Federal-Aid Highway Act authorizes $25 billion to build 41,000 miles of interstate highways.

■ Actress Grace Kelly marries Prince Rainier III of Monaco.

The cover of *Mad* magazine showcases for the first time Alfred E. Neuman's gap-toothed smile and the slogan "What—me worry?"

The Price Is Right, which will eventually set a record for the longest-running game show, premieres.

Yankee pitcher Don Larsen uses a unique no-windup delivery to retire all 27 batters in the first perfect game in a World Series.

Elvis Presley's first RCA record hits music store shelves, and "Elvis mania" begins.

1957

The U.S. detonates its first contained underground nuclear explosion at the Nevada Test Site.

■ *Leave It to Beaver* premieres on CBS.

Escorted by federal troops, nine African-American students, the Little Rock Nine, integrate formerly all-white Central High School in Little Rock, Arkansas.

New products on the market include the transistorized pacemaker and Wham-O's first flying disc (later called the **Frisbee**).

Boston Celtic **Bill Russell** sets an NBA record with 49 rebounds against Philadelphia.

Dick Clark introduces *American Bandstand* to a national audience.

■ Russia begins the space race by launching the first Earth-orbiting satellite, *Sputnik 1*.

■ President Eisenhower takes the oath for his second term.

A whopping 4.3 million babies were born in the U.S. in 1957—the biggest year of the baby boom.

Ford releases the midsize **Edsel**, an epic fail.

1958

- Fourteen-year-old whiz Bobby Fischer wins the U.S. Chess Championship.

- Congress creates NASA.

Unidentified U.S. soldiers killed in WWII and the Korean War are interred at the **Tomb of the Unknown Soldier** in Arlington National Cemetery.

- Pan Am ushers in the Jet Age by offering overseas flights with the Boeing 707.

- Kellogg's introduces Cocoa Krispies, and General Mills debuts Cocoa Puffs.

- The first International House of Pancakes (IHOP) opens in Toluca Lake, California.

- Rock 'n' roll idol Elvis Presley is inducted into the Army.

- The Hula-Hoop and Rice-a-Roni—aka the San Francisco treat—are introduced.

- Italian Cardinal Angelo Roncalli is crowned Pope John XXIII.

The U.S. launches its first satellite, *Explorer 1,* to compete with the Russian *Sputniks*.

1959

- Alaska and Hawaii become states.

- Mattel introduces the Barbie doll.

- *Bonanza* is introduced, and it runs for 14 years.

The world of rock 'n' roll is stunned by the news that **Buddy Holly,** Ritchie Valens and J.P. "The Big Bopper" Richardson Jr. have been killed in a plane crash near Mason City, Iowa.

More than 4,000 **drive-in movie theaters** can be found across the country.

- Wilt "The Stilt" Chamberlain makes his NBA debut with the Philadelphia Warriors.

- Frank Lloyd Wright, the most prominent architect in the U.S., dies.

TV viewers are shocked to learn that *Twenty One* game show winner Charles Van Doren was coached during his appearances on the show.

SCHOOL'S OUT! Eager to enjoy summer vacation in 1954, these students break into a run as they exit school on their last day of reading, writing and arithmetic until classes resume in the fall.

GROWING UP

Life in the 1950s sure was grand,
especially if you were a fresh-faced
kid or a starry-eyed teenager.

Hooked on Fishing

My first fishing experience on a motorboat with my father was in 1952 when I was 10. We were invited to my uncle's cabin on a beautiful lake in northern Michigan.

Being a lifelong hunter and fisherman, my father was a stickler about safety. "There is nothing more important than safety when it comes to fishing or hunting," he told me.

I prepared for our trip by casting in our backyard with a rubber sinker tied to the line on my fishing pole. Targeting a tin bucket, I snapped my line over the back of my head and whipped it forward. My cast often landed near or inside the bucket, so I felt confident and ready for my first fishing trip on a lake.

The sun shone brightly that morning. We walked down to the boat dock and loaded our gear and lunch boxes. My dad cranked the wooden boat's outboard motor and soon we were in the center of the lake, where we dropped anchor.

First thing, Dad told me to bait my hook and cast out about 20 feet. I sat in the front while he prepared his line at the rear. I wanted my first cast to impress my father, but when I whipped my pole back over my head and began my forward thrust, I felt a tug preventing me from completing my cast. At the same time, I heard my father shout for me to drop my rod immediately.

I did exactly as I was told. When I turned around I was shocked at what I saw. My fish hook had embedded in my father's left thigh. He cut the line with his knife, and in as calm a voice as he could muster, he said, "I guess I forgot to teach you not to cast over your head when someone is behind you."

We made it back to shore, where he got the hook out of his leg and bandaged the wound. We rested for a while before returning to the boat to try our luck again. After a bad beginning, the day turned out well; between the two of us, we caught a whole string of fish.

Besides learning another safety rule, I learned something else that day: When it comes to fishing, never let one mess up spoil your whole day.

DONALD L. DEREADT
SHELBY TOWNSHIP, MI

Donald Dereadt takes the wheel of the boat on his first fishing trip with his dad in northern Michigan.

Judy waves as her dad captures her and her mom leaving for school in this first-day photo. Judy keeps the dress she wore that day stored in a cedar chest.

BUT MOM, EVERYBODY HAS ONE!

MY DAD, ALWAYS READY WITH HIS camera, took a picture of me and my mom on my first day of school in 1955. The elementary school in Ozark, Arkansas, was only a hop, skip and a jump from our home, so Mom and I walked there.

I was excited, even eager to start school. My first-grade teacher, Miss Elgin, happened to be my Sunday school teacher, so I was happy and content to be in her classroom.

The first day was only a half day, so we left before lunch. I rushed home to inform my mom that everyone in my class had a book satchel except for me. I was feeling quite indignant, even though I'm now sure that only two or three kids actually had one.

When my dad came home for lunch, I urged him to eat quickly so we could go to the Ben Franklin store and buy a book satchel—which he did.

I thought it was a thing of beauty, my bag: red, with a picture of Alice in Wonderland on it.

That first day of school remains a fond memory for me.

JUDY VAUGHT THORNTON
CLARKSVILLE, AR

KING OF THE APES

I grew up in a small North Dakota town with one movie theater. Nearly every kid was there for the Saturday matinee, usually a Western or a comedy, but my favorites were the Tarzan films.

When I was a second-grader, in 1953, I had just seen a matinee starring the greatest Tarzan of all: Johnny Weissmuller. I entered the boys bathroom at school on Monday, thinking that because the door was heavy, it must be soundproof.

It wasn't. When the door shut, I let out an ear-piercing Tarzan yell—immediately followed by my classmates' uproarious laughter from the other side of the door!

I stayed there as long as my embarrassment allowed and emerged to gales of laughter (even my teacher couldn't help herself). Sixty-some years later, I still look back and blush.
DOUGLAS SLETTEN • MESA, AZ

SLIDING HOME

We had a playmate in North Hollywood, California, in the '50s whose mom worked, so we were not allowed to play in her house during the day, even though she had an older brother and sister. One day her brother figured out a game for us that wasn't played inside the house, so technically it was legal: We would crawl up on top of the open garage door and then someone would close the door so we could slide down. How we managed to do this over and over without decapitating ourselves is beyond me. And, no, I never told my mom.
SUE ANN HILMO
PRESCOTT VALLEY, AZ

THAT 'COCOA' WAS A LITTLE TOO HOT

ONE AFTERNOON IN 1955, WHILE VISITING my grandmother in Albuquerque, New Mexico, I was watching her without her knowing. I was 7 at the time.

I saw her open a drawer in the big desk at the back of the living room, scoop up some chocolate-colored powder from a container and put it in her mouth—or at least that's what I thought she did.

I was sure it was cocoa. And it must have been a very special cocoa, I thought, because she kept it in a secret hiding place.

I really wanted to try it. I decided that Grandma probably wouldn't notice if some of her cocoa was gone, so as soon as she left the room, I crept over to the desk, slid open the drawer and took out the container. I put a bit of the brown powder on my tongue.

And suddenly my mouth was on fire! I screamed and gagged, spilling most of the contents of the container on the floor.

My grandmother and aunt rushed in and, seeing the brown drool on my mouth and the mess on the rug, they both realized what had happened: I had swallowed some of Grandma's snuff tobacco.

Later that evening, when my uncle came home, I heard my aunt telling him what had happened. He laughed and called me into the kitchen.

"Well, Ricky," he said. "How about some cocoa?"

RICK ROSS • SACRAMENTO, CA

Marlene Dietrich, far left, struck a fabulous pose with her cigarette. Carol, pictured near left, was eager to shed her little-girl cuteness for something more Marlene.

A Lesson in Glamour Left Her Gasping

Movie stars made it look so easy to be sophisticated and beautiful.

Back in 1950, when I was 10, there was something I thought I had to learn to do, and the sooner, the better: I wanted to learn how to smoke a cigarette. It seemed glamorous to smoke. Movie stars were glamorous, and didn't they all smoke?

I spent a portion of my weekdays walking to and from our little rural school in Franklin County, Missouri, with my brother Larry and his best friend, Lou. Our long walks gave us plenty of time to make plans—sometimes secret plans.

"How about us teaching you how to smoke?" Lou suggested one day on our walk. He smiled at me, his blue eyes twinkling. Could he read my mind? If he knew I wanted to learn to smoke, did he also know I thought his dimples were absolutely gorgeous?

I kicked a few pebbles out of the path. "I guess that would be all right," I said, trying not to sound too eager.

We chose a beautiful October afternoon for my lesson. The sun was golden and the sky so blue it hurt my eyes. The colored leaves made the world seem like a crunchy rainbow. What a special day this was going to be!

Lou took out a pack of Lucky Strikes and my heart skipped a beat. In just a few minutes I'd be glamorous.

"There's an old log we can sit on," Lou said, pointing to the other side of a fence. We climbed over and perched on the log, a boy sitting on either side of me. I tossed my long brown curls over my shoulder. If I was going to be glamorous, I had to look the part.

Each of the boys tapped a cigarette out of the pack and lit up. I could see they were professionals; learning from them would be a definite plus for me. Giddily, and without much prodding, I reached for a cigarette and put it to my mouth.

"Draw hard," my brother said, "or it won't light." I took a deep breath.

I felt as if I'd inhaled dynamite. My lungs, throat, nose and eyes were searing. This wasn't glamorous. It wasn't even fun! It was awful.

Through a haze of smoky tears, I glared at the boys. Coughing violently, I jumped up and half-fell over the fence in my desperate attempt to escape.

"Hey, wait!" Larry called. But I was in no mood for conversation. I didn't care where they went or what they did or for how long.

I only knew they didn't need to save any more cigarettes for me.

CAROL ROHLFING · HERMANN, MO

Preserving the Tradition

The 1950s were wonderful years to grow up in northern Indiana. I was in high school then, and it was customary that the senior class would play a joke on the principal at the end of the school year. In mid-March, we had a class meeting to discuss Senior Day and the Senior Day joke. A show of hands indicated the majority of the class wasn't into joking. Over the following weekend, I discussed this with two of my brothers and my boyfriend. They agreed that the class of 1955 couldn't walk away from tradition. At the time, I was a short, red-haired, bespectacled girl. A true innocent, or so everyone thought. But as the oldest of four and the only girl, I really had an evil, twisted mind.

My oldest brother was a student coach for the varsity teams and had access to the main part of the school. My middle brother was friends with one of the custodians. They agreed to get me into the main hallway, by the principal's office, and arrange for a ladder to be in that hall on Thursday evening the following week.

At 8:30 that Thursday, my boyfriend and I eased through the door my brother had left ajar for me. The ladder was in place, and the custodian told me which ceiling tile I needed to move to get into the ventilation duct over the principal's office. Less than 10 minutes and the deed was done. We made sure the door was shut before we ran all the way to my house. The next day was April 1. The weather was warmer than usual, and the custodian asked the principal if he should turn on the ventilation system. Good idea! It took about 10 minutes before there was a strange noise swishing through the vents. The principal was running up and down the halls, trying to discover where the noise originated. This went on for the rest of the day.

When we arrived at school on Monday, the principal made an announcement over the intercom. "Were the marbles in the ventilating system the senior-class prank? I want to know who, when and how this prank was carried out. Now!" Of course, no one knew anything. I considered confessing right then, but the principal thought I was quite the angel.

We graduated May 27. I had a speaking part in the ceremony, and when I had finished the approved speech, I said, "Mr. Principal, fellow classmates, I put 500 marbles in the ventilation system over the principal's office on April 1. I felt it was my duty to preserve the tradition." No one believed me, but I had confessed. My conscience was clear.

When I attended the 25th class reunion, the principal shook my hand, then patted it gently and said, "I realized a few weeks after graduation that you probably had played the prank—otherwise how could you know there were 500 marbles?" I just smiled and said, "May I buy you a drink, sir?"

CHARLOTTE LEWIS · VANCOUVER, WA

GILT BEFORE GUILT

WHEN I WAS A JUNIOR AT ROBERTSDALE (Alabama) High School in 1951, my friends Joyce and Doris talked me into skipping school and going to Mobile to celebrate Mardi Gras. I knew playing hooky was wrong, but the thought of such a fun-filled day was just too tempting.

Bubbling over with anticipation, we rode the bus to Mobile, then hit our first parade. We enjoyed watching the dragons spitting fire, as well as all the floats. After cheering for the bands, we ran down side streets in order to see the same parade again.

That afternoon we caught other parades, cheered for King Felix and his lovely queen, and laughed at the Comic Cowboys.

As we walked around, we kept running into other Robertsdale students. I began to feel better about my own truancy, but my conscience kept trying to spoil my day.

Much, much later, we three weary girls trod long blocks to Joyce's mother's apartment in Mobile. Once there we drifted off to sleep, planning to return Wednesday morning before classes started so no one would be the wiser. But we all overslept. We had to take a later bus. And our hearts sank when we finally got to school and realized we must face English with Mrs. Hiles.

We entered with all eyes on us, and slid into our seats. Mrs. Hiles asked us why we'd barged in while class was in progress. Humiliated, we told the truth. We figured our grades were in jeopardy. And we all knew that we had better be model students from then on.

I learned an important lesson that Mardi Gras— I should always let my conscience be my guide. Never again would I be willing to play hooky and face consequences like those.

JEANETTE RYAN · ROBERTSDALE, AL

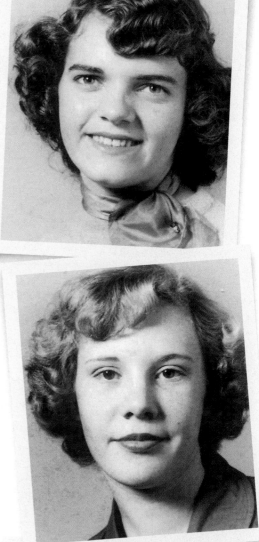

Anything but hooligans, these three high school friends (from top), Jeanette Dyess Ryan, Joyce Gray Willisson and Doris Bonner Clark, played hooky on Mardi Gras.

BOOKS FOR BOOMERS

My second-grade class was bursting with boomer children. I was picked for this photo that ran in the Burlington, Wisconsin, newspaper to represent a typical 1950s child in front of books we'd be using throughout grade school. A sign of the times: My companion, Dell Geise, died in Vietnam.

ARDYTH GILDING WYLLER
SHERWOOD, OR

SEEN THROUGH A HAWKEYE
I took this picture of my friends Louis Schneider and Les Lumbattis with their push racer in Maywood, California, in about 1950, using my fixed-focus Brownie.
DON CUNNINGHAM • CERES, CA

GOING FOR A STROLL
My sister, Eva Maria (right), and I loved playing with our dolls back in 1957. We're in front of our house in Red Hill, Pennsylvania, ready to take the dolls for a ride in the doll buggy.
KARIN DERR RASMUSSEN
GRASS VALLEY, CA

PATRIOTIC COWBOY
Growing up in the Woodside section of Queens, New York, my friends and I made a mini United Nations, and woe to me if I refused to play with anyone. My dad took this picture on July 4, circa 1954. It shows just how real the melting pot image of America was—and that my urban cowboy look was good for getting the girls.
LOUIS A. ALT JR. • UNION, NJ

Toy Time!

Popular 1950s toys morphed into cultural mainstays.

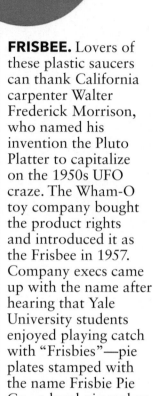

Some of the most memorable toys ever made hit the market in the 1950s, buoyed by a post-war consumer boom that gave marketers their first tantalizing glimpse of a consumption-minded colossus: the baby boomers.

While their prosperous parents snapped up color TVs and turquoise-blue appliances, youngsters clutching allowances turned toys like Frisbees and Hula-Hoops into pop-culture icons. Another powerful duo fueled these toys' wild popularity: television advertising and Madison Avenue marketing firms, where men in gray flannel suits convened over three-martini lunches, hatching plans to sell toys in unimaginable numbers. Boy, did they ever.

Here are some enduring favorites:

BARBIE. Introduced in 1959, Barbie was both revered and reviled over the decades for her shapely hourglass figure. The brainchild of Mattel Inc. co-founder Ruth Handler, the 11½-inch-tall plastic fashionista originally wore a black-and-white striped swimsuit, high-heeled shoes and gold hoop earrings. Named for Handler's daughter, Barbie first sold for $3; a vintage, mint-condition, boxed Barbie now sells for thousands of dollars.

FRISBEE. Lovers of these plastic saucers can thank California carpenter Walter Frederick Morrison, who named his invention the Pluto Platter to capitalize on the 1950s UFO craze. The Wham-O toy company bought the product rights and introduced it as the Frisbee in 1957. Company execs came up with the name after hearing that Yale University students enjoyed playing catch with "Frisbies"—pie plates stamped with the name Frisbie Pie Co., a local pie-maker. They changed the spelling to avoid legal entanglements, and Frisbees have been flying high ever since.

TONKA TOYS.
Little boys bent on destruction met their match in these virtually indestructible vehicles, originally built from automobile-gauge steel. Formally sold under the Tonka Toys name in 1955, the ubiquitous banana yellow dump trucks, bulldozers and graders were more common in backyards than pink flamingos. The name Tonka (a Dakota-Sioux word

that means "great") comes from Lake Minnetonka, which was visible from the company's first manufacturing facility in Minnesota.

PEZ. Austrian Eduard Hass II initially created Pez as a mint candy to help smokers kick the habit—hence the cigarette lighter-like dispenser. The name was derived from the German word for peppermint: PfeffErminZ. In the early 1950s, the treat was introduced in the U.S. as a fruit-flavored candy with dispensers topped by goofy cartoonish heads. It was a smoking-hot idea; consumers still devour the candies and collect the dispensers.

HULA-HOOP.
An epidemic of the hippy-hippy shakes hit America big-time in 1958, when the toy whizzes at Wham-O introduced brightly colored plastic Hula-Hoops after learning that Australian children were gaga about shaking bamboo hoops around their hips. Popular? You bet, Daddio. Consumers bought more than 100 million at $1.98 a pop during the first year alone.

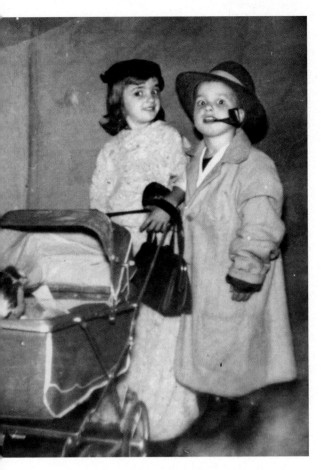

Pushing the baby in a carriage, Kenney and his sister, Donise, are dressed for a stroll.

SOME THINGS NEVER CHANGE

MY OLDER SISTER AND I WERE ABOUT 6 and 7 in this 1957 photo (above) taken in Houston, Texas. As usual, we were playing together. I'm not sure who wanted to be married, but I suspect it was Sister. We often put on Mom's and Dad's clothes to play house and dragged our baby doll in the carriage wherever we went.

Sometimes we pretended we owned a business called Ken's Cafe, since my name is Kenney. As far back as I can remember, Sister called me Papa and I called her Mama. To this day, we still call each other by those nicknames when we talk or write.

Our mother, in her 80s, says we'll never grow up. Family holidays are usually filled with our nonstop laughter and plenty of jokes between us and our younger twin brothers. Remembering the old days is one of our favorite things to do. As they say, some things never change!

KENNEY SLATTEN • AMARILLO, TX

DEAR DIARY

MY PINK PLASTIC-COVERED DIARY came with a short message inside: "Christmas 1957, with love, Mother."

I hadn't thought about that book in decades until I found it buried in a dresser drawer. The worn cover showing a young ponytailed girl transported me back to the year I was 10.

The diary still sported its lock but was missing the key that had kept my writings secret. My first entry was on New Year's Day 1958. After that, I included stories about school days and my teacher Sister Maureen Ann.

One entry tells how Sister Maureen Ann asked me to go outside and burn test papers in the burn barrel. She even gave me matches to start the fire. I wrote that I was scared because Mother didn't let me use matches. I wonder if I ever told her about that experience. Maybe I had secrets after all.

Unfortunately, my daily writings ended on Feb. 16. Not a very good showing.

If my mother were still here, I would thank her for giving me that diary so I could relive a few events from 1958.

GLORIA GRIEPENSTROH
EVANSTON, IN

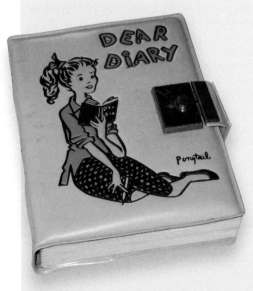

Tall girl Wynne was all smiles at her junior prom in 1955 with her date, Don Donoon, a clear 6-footer.

The Tall Tale Heart-to-Heart

She tried to be helpful, but the stern Miss Davenport came up short.

No one was tall when I was growing up—not anyone who mattered to me, at least. In grade school I was continually placed in the back row for class pictures. At 11, I had to take my birth certificate to the movies to get the 12-and-younger discount.

By the 1950s, at 14, I had reached my full height of just under 6 feet. Towering over the masses, I was invariably the last chosen in those horrible team sports in gym class. In the school play, I was never the ingenue, but the spinster schoolteacher.

When it came to clothes, I was resigned to have a wardrobe with waistlines out of sync with my actual waist and sleeves that stopped just south of the elbow. One-piece bathing suits had me doubled over at a severe angle.

I tried to find solace in Gwen Davenport's *The Tall Girl's Handbook*, but Miss Davenport had a knack for what might be called tough love. She dished out "common sense and sound advice" and more than a few stern admonishments: "No ruffles or cuteness or anything suggestive of the southern belle, no masculine-looking suits with pencil-straight skirts and severely tailored lapels, no padded shoulders, lest you look like a football tackle.

And no trousers!" So that left, what—ball gowns and muumuus?

All the rules that apply to other girls apply doubly to tall girls, Miss Davenport wrote: "Dirty fingernails look worse on a big hand." I took this advice to heart.

Boys? It was all about height. And Miss Davenport was certainly no help on that front. "If you sometimes feel lonely because you have no date when your shorter counterparts do, be on guard against falling into association with misfits and neurotics."

Would you believe that in 1959 the tall girl was told that just as your clothes have to fit you, so should your house? Not for us the quaint colonial saltbox with 6-foot ceilings.

I ended up marrying someone who is 6 feet 3 inches. We had four daughters, all of them short. I have lived happily in an average house with average ceilings. I drive a VW Bug—petite and bright red.

So for all Miss Davenport's not-so-sound advice, she was right about one thing: "To be abnormally tall," she wrote, "is not to be abnormal in any significant way."

WYNNE CROMBIE
HUNTLEY, IL

S IS FOR STUBBORN—AND SHREWD

Mama was determined to give them the World.

ALTHOUGH I DON'T RECALL MY PARENTS ever saying "I love you," there was one night when my mama did something that showed me that she loved me very much.

It was in 1956, when I was 9, and we lived in Manchester, Tennessee. Daddy was shouting "Git 'em!" to the Lone Ranger and Tonto on the TV when someone knocked on the door.

Mama opened it to a salesman with a large sample case. "I would like to show you the best collection of knowledge in the world," he told her. "The epitome of erudition."

Daddy squeezed in next to Mama and said, "We don't need that." He tried to muscle past her to shut the door, but Mama stopped him. She invited the man in.

He took out four books, passing one each to Mama, me, my 6-year-old sister, Barbara, and Daddy, though Daddy wouldn't take his. The man explained that there were 19 volumes in the World Book encyclopedia set. "And each year for five years, starting in January, you get an update," he said.

"What do they cost?" Mama asked.

"You pay $10 down and $6 a month."

Suspicious, Daddy asked, "Altogether what do they cost?"

"It's $170 with special binding, but if you can't afford that, we have regular binding for $120." When Daddy looked shocked, the salesman added, "Remember your children. Aren't they worth that—their education?"

Daddy scoffed. He had no schooling and he was doing all right, he said. "I got a house, food on the table, a mill, a car."

Mama tried to shush him. She watched me leafing through my book, stopping to look at pictures and read an entry or two. Mama made up her mind.

"I want them for the girls," she announced, and when Daddy tried to protest, she added, "I'll pay for them." She would use the money she earned at the shoe factory. The salesman hurried to dig out his paperwork.

Daddy argued that he needed Mama's money to help pay for the land he was buying for his sawmill. She ignored him, signed the papers, and gave the salesman a $10 bill.

Six weeks later, I got home from school to find three big boxes on the porch.

"They're here, Mama!"

She cleared out a cabinet and we loaded it with the volumes in alphabetical order. I opened the F book and saw pictures of Cahors, France. "When I grow up, I'm going there," I said. "You can go with me."

"That far?" Mama replied. "How about you take me to Nashville, to the Grand Ole Opry?"

"OK. Is that in the G volume?"

"Look it up."

BRANDIE WARREN · SMYRNA, TN

Mary Anie, Brandie's mama, wisely invited the encyclopedia salesman in for a chat.

Sights and Sounds
That Left Them Speechless

In 1952, there were 17 in my graduating class in Lawton, Michigan. Some of us had started kindergarten together, and even with add-ons and drop-offs, we were a fairly close-knit bunch. Perhaps because we had a history together or because we were an adventurous lot, we decided to take a senior trip upon graduation. Now, the usual senior trip was a day at a Lake Michigan beach or an overnight stay in Chicago. Our trip plans were more ambitious than our bank balance. Even after fundraising, all seniors had to chip in extra through their own industriousness or generous parents.

We had decided to take a school bus to Washington, D.C., for over a week but first had to obtain permission from the school board and prepare a detailed schedule so our travels could be tracked. And so, along with our class adviser as principal driver, we left Lawton.

No words can describe the wonder of Washington for a group of small-town seniors. We went to Ford's Theatre, where we traced the footsteps of Lincoln's assassin and visited the museum below. We toured the Capitol and learned about a spot on the Rotunda floor where one can hear what others on the other side are saying—a matter of acoustics. The Lincoln Memorial certainly was one of the most impressive sights. We spent time at the Smithsonian Institution and the National Cathedral, possibly the most awe-inspiring place we visited. We were impressed by the vastness and solemnity of the Arlington National Cemetery and the Tomb of the Unknown Soldier.

We arrived back at the school bus garage with family and friends waiting to greet us. We were a tired but happy lot, not truly realizing the significance of the experience we had just shared.

SALLY R. HAINLINE · LAWTON, MI

Friendship is the best ship: Members of the class of 1952 flash a big smile before taking Washington, D.C., by storm.

William, in bow tie, drummed up support for Ike at a mock election at Wilson High in West Lawn, Pennsylvania, in 1952. Below is the mock election committee.

THEY LIKED IKE, TOO

AS ELECTION DAY 1952 APPROACHED, OUR high school planned an assembly that would include a mock election. Students were chosen to speak on behalf of each candidate: Dwight Eisenhower (Republican), Adlai Stevenson (Democrat) and Darlington Hoopes (Socialist). I was selected to give the speech for Eisenhower.

I even grew a mustache for the event.

The mock candidate committees went to the real local campaign headquarters for each party, where we loaded up on pins, banners, posters, pictures, hats—anything related to the election we could use to decorate the school auditorium.

On the day of the assembly, the music teacher led the band in patriotic songs, and speeches were punctuated with loud cheers and clapping. I ended my speech by shouting into the microphone, "Vote for Dwight D. Eisenhower, the next president of the United States!" Red, white and blue balloons dropped from the balcony as my Republican supporters cheered.

Our mock ballot went to Eisenhower by a wide margin, as did the real ballot in the general election.

WILLIAM KULP • YORK, PA

MIRROR MIRROR
Prom was a new experience for **PERLETTE ALVAREZ,** now of Reno, Nevada. She immigrated to the U.S. and became a citizen in 1952. Her prom was in Lincoln, Nebraska, in '56.

FAIR FOOD
In the 1950s, the most exciting high school band trip for me was the October trek from our school in San Augustine, Texas, to Shreveport, Louisiana, to march in the parade that officially opened the huge fair now known as the State Fair of Louisiana. We were always dressed in our spiffy red and white band uniforms, with spending money from our parents stuffed in our pockets.

I was introduced to cotton candy there as well as soft ice cream. The ice cream was much like the soft serve at a Dairy Queen, but it was a new item at the time. I always ended up with several small loaves of white bread, which I took home to enjoy later.

I haven't returned to that fair since then. I suppose I'd need to be dressed in a band uniform to feel at home.
NEAL MURPHY
SAN AUGUSTINE, TX

SECOND GRADE

THIRD GRADE

FIFTH GRADE

SIXTH GRADE

SEVENTH GRADE

EIGHTH GRADE

DAD'S BACK-TO-SCHOOL HAIRCUTS

Reader **JUDY SIPE** of York, Pennsylvania, reminded us that back in the day, pro haircuts for kids were not the norm. "I didn't go to a hairdresser until my senior year of high school. My dad always cut our hair," she wrote. Well done, Dad. Your daughter is as cute as a button in every pose!

Wearing his cowboy outfit, Tex was able to sit outside on the swings during his long hospital stay.

This Buckaroo Had Spirit and Spunk

After contracting polio, he countered the unknown with laughter and faith.

Prior to July 1953, I was a healthy, active boy who played tag and baseball with my younger brother and friends and roller-skated down the streets of my hometown in eastern Iowa. But every summer across America, families kept careful watch for symptoms of the polio virus.

One fateful day when I was 7, I woke up with a backache and a high fever. My parents rushed me to Guttenberg Hospital, about 10 miles away. Within minutes, I was put in an ambulance with my mother and taken to Dubuque Hospital, where we transferred to another ambulance and went to the children's hospital in Iowa City.

There, Dr. Collins, a polio specialist, told my parents that I had contracted the dreaded disease, for which there was no cure. This was the beginning of a life of unknowns. No one knew how the virus spread or how to stop it.

For the next 100 days, I stayed in a ward with rows of beds and iron lungs. My fever broke after four days, but all the strength in my legs and lower back was gone. I received various treatments, including strips of hot lamb's wool applied to my legs several times a day.

My mother rented a room near the hospital to be close to me until the stress became too much for her. My father would drive the 200-mile round trip on dirt roads to see me.

I spent my eighth birthday in the hospital. My parents got me a cowboy outfit and everyone called me Tex. I was the kid in the hospital who made all the doctors, nurses and other children in the ward laugh.

About six months after I went home, Jonas Salk began conducting widespread trials for the polio vaccine. I don't have to look far to see people who are far worse off than me. My prayer is that I can make a difference in other people's lives by making them smile.

ARTHUR "TEX" WILLMAN
SPRING HILL, FL

❝

Here are my two kids, Neal and Sue, along with their friend Gena, at the base of a long toboggan run at Mount Pinos, California, in 1952. Neal turned out to be a very good skier.

HARRY JUNGI · OROVILLE, CA

WINTER COMPETITIONS

Sledding was a big part of our playtime in Michigan's Upper Peninsula. In this 1956 photo, I'm on the sled next to my brothers Jeff (left) and Steve (far right) and our friend Vernon Kokko. We lived on a hill and spent hours seeing who was fastest or who could force whom into a snowbank.

KEN LINNA · SOUTH RANGE, MI

A VERY DISNEY FAMILY

In 1955, my dad (third from the left) moved our family from Minnesota so he could work as a painter at Disneyland. I also got a job, working on Main Street, where I met my future husband, who worked at the Red Wagon Inn. Years later, my daughter was hired as a ride operator!

JANET McMANUS · COLORADO SPRINGS, CO

MEETING WALT

At 12, I was lucky enough to see Disneyland when it opened in 1955. One of the Main Street, U.S.A. employees told me that Walt Disney enjoyed riding the Mark Twain riverboat in Frontierland. Eager to see in person the man I knew from Sunday TV, I went looking and found him on the upper foredeck. I nervously approached him, held out my parking stub, and asked for his autograph. "Do you think it's as easy as that?" he asked. I stammered with uncertainty, but he smiled and said, "It is," reaching his hand out for the ticket. Half a century later, I have no idea what happened to my signed souvenir, but my moment with Walt has not faded.

CHARLIE PYEATTE
CHANDLER, AZ

A MECHANICAL HIPPO ATE HIS SWORD

In 1957, I was 9, and my family took a road trip from Montana to California to visit Disneyland. It was our first day in the park, and I remember almost immediately buying a Zorro sword at the souvenir stand.

One of our first adventures was going on the Jungle Cruise. As you're going down this river maze, crocodiles and other animals come off the shore and rise out of the water with their jaws wide open. When a hippo came up, our boat operator pulled his revolver out of his holster and shot into the hippo's mouth; the hippo plunged under the water again.

I was in the back of the boat when a hippo popped up with his open jaws. I jabbed him in his mouth with my Zorro sword, but before I knew it, the sword had been pulled out of my hand, and the hippo went back under with my sword still in his mouth. I was devastated that that crummy hippo stole my sword, and I never did get a new one.

STEVE MATZ · BILLINGS, MT

Walt Disney created his namesake theme park in 1955 for $17.5 million.

Vintage Ads

Decorating a potato head and drinking sugary green liquid was the norm for kids back in the '50s.

1953

THE NEWLYWEDS—Mr. and Mrs. Potato Head—were touted as one of the top toys for Christmas in 1953.

1959

ORIGINALLY KNOWN as the Pitcher Man, the Kool-Aid Man and his grin first graced the soft drink's ads in 1954. Just try to tear your eyes away from that hypnotic green gaze!

LAYAWAY KITTEN

Because my brother and I asked that Tabby be set aside for us while he was still weaning, we thought of him as our layaway. Later we trained him to take a doll's bottle, as in this 1958 photo taken at our home in Pennsylvania.

KATHY HEAD McDONALD · ALBION, PA

STARDUST MEMORIES

My friends and I rarely wanted to be off our horses. Once, a local riding instructor set up an Easter egg hunt with treats hidden where we could reach them from our saddles. Here I am with Stardust in 1953, when I was 12.

JUDY PEARCE · CARPINTERIA, CA

THE LOYAL SOLDIER

My brother Charles and dog Blackie took me to class every morning and saw me home. Here are my protectors in 1951—they gave me so much love.

LIBBY ORENDORFF · DICKINSON, TX

THE LAKE WAS THE PLACE TO GO

ICE-SKATING ON "THE LAKE," AS IT was called, between Harrison and Lake streets on South 14th in Lincoln, Nebraska, was an incredibly popular winter outing for young people. On any given Saturday in winter, kids from all directions gathered at The Lake to play on the ice. The city built a warming shelter there in the late 1950s, complete with a wood-burning fireplace and a pile of stacked wood just for the kids to use to keep the fire stoked.

The Lake was a natural depression on the west end of Irvingdale Park. The city flooded it only occasionally. A warm winter sun followed by a hard freeze overnight generally provided the next day's icy smooth surface, perfect for skaters. The Lake comprised about 1 acre, with a small island and one big weeping willow tree.

In the 1950s a pair of skates was as much a part of a kid's possessions as a cellphone is today. We enjoyed every kind of ice-skating activity: figure skating, around-the-island speed races, hockey, barrel jumping or even, at times, the hazardous crack-the-whip, and we did it all unsupervised.

DON C. FICKE
PLEASANT DALE, NE

A Little Good Humor

The Good Humor man and my brother, Rick, were friends. In this photo taken in 1950 near our house in Lake Mahopac, New York, Pete let Rick, 2, take the wheel of his truck. Those were the best times. When we heard the bells of Pete's truck, we'd all come running. An ice cream cost 15 cents back then, but if we didn't have money, we'd all sing loud so we couldn't hear the bells.
RUTH LEACH · BRICK, NJ

A SERVICEMAN views a television program with his family at the U.S. Air Force base near Limestone, Maine, in 1954. TV watching was becoming the great American pastime in homes of the 1950s.

ALL IN THE FAMILY

Suburban subdivisions popped up everywhere, and baby boomers became catalysts of change.

Fern and Ray's kids Anita Faye and Leslie Ray stood out with their red hair, but they were no match for a colorful news story.

They Were Grateful Four Times Over

Red-haired siblings had to mind their p's and q's, until the Ponder Quads changed everything.

When Daddy became the new pastor in Murfreesboro, Arkansas, population 1,075, he warned my brother Leslie Ray and me that our behavior would be watched and reported around town.

We would have loved to dig for diamonds over at the crater, for instance. Years earlier someone had found diamonds in the dirt on a farm outside town, and the property had become a tourist attraction. You paid a fee to search for diamonds all day, and what you found you kept. But Daddy said it wasn't becoming for the preacher's kids to be out there digging for profit. (The site is now Crater of Diamonds State Park, and the finders-keepers policy still applies.)

It didn't help that we were the only kids with red hair in our church. We were constantly noticed when what we wanted most was to blend in. Lucky for us, our town was on the brink of change with an event that would distract attention from two freckled redheads.

On Jan. 14, 1952, the Ponder family instantly expanded by four with the birth of quadruplets: Donna Fay, Danny Kay, Dewey Ray and Dickey Gay. Dr. Duncan delivered the babies at the cabin where Mr. and Mrs. Ponder lived with their eight other children. The Ponder Quads, as everyone started calling them, were big news

in town, and a newspaper reporter interviewed the family. The story said the Ponders didn't have enough chairs to sit on; they hadn't had enough for their children even before the quadruplets were born.

"Well, I never," Daddy said when he read the article. "We have to get that family what they need."

But before he could get his charity effort going, the Ponders had become famous, and businesses began to give them all they needed. The quaduplets were photographed with Pet evaporated milk, and the company built the family a new house with a wall-to-wall window in the front room so the public could see the babies. Now the whole nation could point and stare without being considered unkind. Mr. and Mrs. Ponder went to New York City to be on television.

The Ponder Quads did my brother and me a great big favor. While they were lying around being famous, we could fade into the background, getting away with mischief. The town turned out to have exceeded our hopes and dreams. As far as we were concerned, there couldn't be a better place to live in 1952 than Murfreesboro—new population 1,079.

ANITA GARNER
SACRAMENTO, CA

A TASTE OF THE PAST

Mom's old faithful stirs up memories of beloved family meals.

ONE RECENT COLD, SNOWY DAY, while searching for a soup recipe, I stumbled across a cookbook with a faded red cover, worn edges and broken binding. It was my mother's old faithful: *Betty Crocker's Picture Cook Book,* copyright 1950.

I chuckled over pictures in the "How to Prepare" section. Hand-mixing, chopping, grating and shredding—no food processors back then. Stovetop melting, caramelizing and dissolving—no microwave either.

I stopped at a soiled page called "Favorite Pancakes." Here was our family's No. 1 destination for Sunday breakfast choices. We'd rush home from church, and everyone would pitch in with breakfast. Mom mixed the pancakes and Dad flipped them. We siblings took turns squeezing the orange juice, frying the bacon or sausage, setting the table and washing dishes afterward. That's right, no dishwasher.

A week or so before a birthday, Mom would ask, "What kind of cake do you want?" We had a universe of cakes to choose from, but our favorites never changed. My sister Rosemary and brother Tony invariably replied, "Banana cake with chocolate frosting." So it wasn't surprising that the page headed "Banana Cake" was one of the most food-splattered. I imagined yellow bananas turning brown on the countertop in preparation for my siblings' special days, and I could almost smell the aroma of those bananas as the cake baked.

My favorite cake, marble chiffon, and my brother Frank's favorite, poppy seed, weren't in the cookbook. Mom had cut those recipes from the newspaper.

Dad's favorite dessert was lemon meringue pie, so I knew why food fingerprints smudged the "Pie Crust" page—no store-bought crusts at our house. I could see Mom rolling the dough, carefully placing it in a pie plate and crimping the edges. The page for lemon meringue pie held an obvious clue that the recipe had been a winner: a hole in the center where it had stuck to the previous page. My lips puckered as I remembered the pie's sweet tartness.

Every crinkled, food-smeared page dished up delicious memories—German potato salad for picnics, eggnog at Christmas and mac and cheese on Lenten Fridays.

Picturing the family gathered around our old Formica-and-chrome kitchen table, eating and sharing fun times, truly warmed my heart that frosty winter day.

LENORE PETRUSO • O'FALLON, MO

Lenore's mother, Lois, cooked up happy times with help from Betty Crocker.

East Coast Explorations

At Niagara Falls, Jim (left) hung out with his cool California cousins, Mark and Ken, sporting rolled-up shirtsleeves and denim cuffs.

Back in 1956, my Uncle Walt and my cousins Mark and Ken drove from California to my home in Aurora, Illinois, to begin an unforgettable tour to the East Coast with me and my dad, Les. Uncle Walt drove a '54 Mercury station wagon that hauled us and our luggage.

The adult brothers sat up front. Ken sat on the split middle seat with his comic books, and Mark and I had the flat open space in the "way back"—no seat belts, and only open windows to cool us.

Our trip took us to Detroit to see Ford automobiles being assembled at the gigantic River Rouge Complex. Then we went to the Henry Ford Museum and Greenfield Village. After that it was on through Canada to Niagara Falls.

My dad and Uncle Walt were pretty frugal with our spending money, so in New York City we stayed at the YMCA with a bathroom down the hall. No problem, and it was still a big deal to us boys. We rode the Staten Island Ferry, visited the top of the Empire State Building, and watched the Rockettes at Radio City Music Hall. (I wonder whose idea that was?)

Street life became a little too real one night when a diminutive drunk tried to pick a fight with 6-foot-2, 220-pound bodybuilder Ken.

We saw the boardwalk in Atlantic City, and then we traveled to Washington, D.C. I remember visiting the Smithsonian Castle and walking unchallenged through all parts of the Capitol and the White House. We then took the Pennsylvania Turnpike to Gettysburg.

As we headed home on the new Indiana toll road, I was impressed that Dad and Uncle Walt allowed us to stay at a Howard Johnson's motel. It was state-of-the-art then.

Two weeks after we started, our marvelous road trip was over. I can't tell you if we cousins caused our fathers any aggravation. I'd rather remember that we didn't. If we did, I regret it, because I am eternally grateful that Dad and Uncle Walt made the loving effort to give us that priceless experience.

Some 60 years later, my memories are still vivid. I think that if I live to be 100, they will remain so.

JIM DOHREN · DAVENPORT, FL

From far left, tailgating cousins Mark, Jim and Ken had Uncle Walt calling the shots. At near left, Ken is unfazed by the monuments and memorials found at Gettysburg National Military Park, while Mark and Jim perch on a cannon.

DAYS OF PERCH AND SUNSHINE

When I was about 12, my Aunt Florence and Uncle Steve retired from their home in Evanston, Illinois, to a small cottage in Green Lake, Wisconsin. Nothing was more pleasing to me than spending time up there with them during my summer vacations.

Fishing was the mainstay of my visits. I'd go out nearly every morning with Uncle Steve and Uncle Homer, who also lived nearby, in Homer's boat, dangling worms in the warm sunshine. We almost always caught something. I recall a time when Uncle Steve brought up a huge catfish, the first one I had ever seen, and it fascinated me. He tossed it back, though, explaining that catfish weren't keepers, at least not in that part of the country. What we were after, he said, were perch or sunfish.

One special day, I caught two perch. I couldn't wait to get back to have my picture taken with those fish and my favorite aunt. I even cleaned them myself!

JAN McCANLESS · CHINA GROVE, NC

Hugged by her Aunt Florence, Jan shows off her morning's handiwork in Green Lake, Wisconsin, in 1955.

SANTA'S SUMMER HOME

Long ago and far away, there was a theme park called Santa's Village in Scotts Valley, California. It was open from 1957 to about 1979, before it closed because of bankruptcy.

Our family visited the park (right) in 1958 when I was 6. We lived in San Jose at the time and often traveled to Santa Cruz on day trips. The park was easy to see from Highway 17 and we passed it every trip.

I loved going to the park but remember being confused about Santa Claus being there in the summertime.

GARY W. QUADROS · KELOWNA, BC

PRICE OF
THE GOOD LIFE

At home, amid concerns of the Korean
War, young couples continued their
migration to new homes. Many of these
houses were prefabricated and located
in outlying areas of their communities.
This lifestyle added a new word to the
nation's vocabulary—"suburbia."

The typical suburban house was ranch-style,
generally with two bedrooms and an attic
that could be converted to two more
bedrooms and a bath. Prices ranged
from about $8,000 to $11,500—with
major appliances usually included.

Those prices were typical on the East
Coast. On the West Coast—in Seattle, for
example—you could buy a home built of
masonry block for $4,999, including the lot.

In most areas of the country, you could get
a government-guaranteed mortgage for a
5 percent down payment (veterans didn't
have to put anything down), with 30 years to
pay. The monthly payment came to about $56.

To furnish that home, you needed to budget
your money so you could buy big-ticket
items—such as a two-piece living room suite
for $157, a seven-piece dining room set for
$149 or a three-piece bedroom set for $139!

THE MAGIC BOX

WRESTLING MATCHES WERE AMONG MY FAMILY'S
favorite things to watch on TV when we got our first set
around 1950. They were new to us, and very different
from our ordinary farm life.

My dad decided that his father would enjoy the sport,
too, so he invited Grandpa and Grandma over for
supper and television. After we had eaten, they were
given the seats of honor, the two rocking chairs directly
in front of the TV.

Grandpa settled back in his chair, stretched his long
legs out and puffed quietly on his pipe. Grandma, too,
relaxed in her chair, rocking gently while talking about
all the fuss over this newfangled television thing.

Once the match started, the only sound in the room
came from the TV. I think my parents and I spent as much
time watching my grandparents as we did the TV.

By the time the match was over, Grandpa was sitting
on the edge of his chair, leaning forward with his arms
on his knees. His forgotten pipe was upside down in his
hand, a little pile of ashes on the floor between his feet.
He wasn't a big talker, but as he slowly came back to
reality, the gleam in his eyes spoke volumes.

Grandma, seldom at a loss for words, had a little trouble
this time. Sitting upright, her eyes very wide, she finally
sputtered, "Why, why, so naughty!"

At that, my parents,
Grandpa and I burst
out laughing.

The evening was a success,
and it wasn't long before
my grandparents bought
their own television.

JEAN AHLSCHLAGER
IONA, MN

WHEN THERE'S NO AC

Jack Gross, second from left, took guests Grant, Neita and Derril Gwinner on a picnic in Columbus, Nebraska, in 1958. Wife Hilvie snapped the shot, sent by daughter **DULCIE SHOENER,** now of Whitefish Bay, Wisconsin, who's pushing sister Melanie's buggy.

RIDING HIGH

My sister Debbie balances on Dad's arm at a gathering in northeastern Ohio in about 1952. I'm the 2-year-old on the blanket with our parents, Kenneth and Magdalen Freeman.
THOMAS FREEMAN
PHOENIX, AZ

On the Spot with Virtuoso

The great pianist displays a talent for acting.

Sitting at the old upright piano in my bedroom, I'm about to play one of the few simple pieces I have mastered—barely a cut above "Twinkle, Twinkle Little Star." I have my best blue dress on and ribbons in my pigtails. Sprawled on the rug keeping an eye on things are our cocker spaniel Rusty and her black-furred son and sidekick, Dusty.

It's cocktail hour in 1950s St. Francisville, Louisiana, and several musicians and guests of the board of the Baton Rouge Symphony Orchestra mingle in our living room. Daddy, highball in hand, leans against the door of my room, smiling with pride.

"You can do it, Annie," he says, with his usual fatherly deaf ear to my flaws. His favorite music at the time was Broadway show tunes, judging by the number of times we had to listen to *South Pacific* on the record player. (Whenever I hear snippets of it, I think of him.)

My mother, whose musical taste is more highfalutin, hovers nearby. Recently she'd taken my Brownie troop to Baton Rouge to see the orchestra, a first for most of my country classmates. One girl from rural Hardwood spotted the cellos and squealed, "Look at them big guitars, y'all!"

Back in my bedroom, I'm cornered. Standing close to me is an elegant Spanish woman in a silk dress, her raven hair pulled back in a bun. On her distinguished face is what can only be called a forced smile. She is world-renowned classical pianist Amparo Iturbi, best known for duets with her brother José. A few years before, the Iturbis had performed Mozart's *Concerto for Two Pianos and Orchestra in E-Flat* in New York City before a crowd of 12,000.

Now, as the visiting performer with the orchestra, Amparo Iturbi is our guest, compelled to listen to…me. It must be agony for her. A prodigy I am not. As I rush through the piece—more *presto* than stately *lento*—even the dogs shamble out of the room.

Fortunately for everyone, but especially for Madame Iturbi, my recital is brief. She claps politely and says, "*Brava!*"

We have both put on a worthy performance.

ANNE SEMMES · CHARLESTON, SC

The author's father on the *Pegasus* during the San Diego-to-Acapulco yacht race.

LOST AT SEA

IN 1958, MY DAD entered our 38-foot gaff-rigged schooner, the *Pegasus,* in the San Diego-to-Acapulco yacht race, a distance of 1,430 nautical miles. Our boat was the smallest in the race, and I, at age 13, was the youngest person.

The start was so exciting—we heard the shot, and we were off! Dad would navigate by celestial navigation using a sextant, maps and charts, and a stopwatch (no GPS in those days).

My father sincerely believed in celestial navigation, so he could not understand why, every morning, we were 20 miles farther offshore than we were supposed to be. He finally found out that one of the crew members could not see the compass at night and had decided to follow a star, taking us 200 miles off course.

About three days later, disaster struck. We went into the doldrums—no wind at all. We motored until we ran out of fuel. Dad tried to radio for help, but the battery was dead. There we sat, no wind, no motor and no radio. It was grim.

After a couple of days, we saw a speck on the horizon. Thank God, it was an oil freighter, offering help! The crew lowered a rope ladder for us to use to climb aboard. The captain greeted us and said he always stopped when he saw a small boat out that far. He then sent mechanics down to fill our tanks with fuel and put a new battery in the radio. We went on our way with the freighter checking on us every day by radio.

When we finally arrived in Acapulco, the race committee said it was getting a search-and-rescue party ready to leave the next day to look for us. When we returned home after touring Mexico City, we learned that our rescue had made the news.

DARLENE THOMPSON VAN HEMELRYCK
PAGE, AZ

Vintage Ads

Keeping one's family clean and dressed and in a good sturdy pair of shoes was important for a 1950s housewife.

No-Rinse chemicals hard on _your_ hands? Join the women who say—

FOR WHITE WHITE WASHES _WITHOUT_ RED HANDS "I'VE GONE BACK TO DUZ!"

DUZ GIANT ECONOMY SIZE

NOW! The Whitest Washes Possible With **Any** Soap!

Yet DUZ gives you almost toilet-soap mildness for your hands!

ONLY DUZ—of _all_ leading washday products—gives you this combination of rich, real soap and two active detergents! And now Duz has more magic whitening power than ever—the most you can get in _any_ soap made!

THAT'S WHY DUZ gives you the cleanest, whitest, brightest washes you can get with _any_ soap on earth!

THAT'S WHY DUZ is milder, kinder to your hands than _any_ other leading washday package soap sold anywhere!

DUZ DOES EVERYTHING
WORKS WONDERS IN EV'RY TYPE WASHING MACHINE!

Says Mrs. Anne McMann of Totowa Boro, N. J.: "I must admit I tried some of those no-rinse chemicals—until I saw what they were doing to my hands! Now I'm back to Duz because it does my wash the way I like it done—clean, fresh and sweet-smelling—and leaves my hands soft and smooth!"

Says her neighbor, Mrs. Claire Brown: "My experiments with no-rinse chemicals taught me just one thing: Never try to do without Duz! Now that I'm back to Duz, I find it gets my towels and sheets and pillow cases even whiter than it did before—and it's still as mild and kind to hands as ever!"

1952

LAUNDRY SOAPS rode a wave of innovation during World War II when the military requested a cleanser that could hold up to seawater. That's where high-powered detergents came in. Duz was known for the glassware and china included as a bonus in each box.

America's Finest Soles

AVONITE _gives_ **EXTRA MONTHS** OF WEAR

AVONITE SOLES

SOLEMARK of QUALITY

TRADE MARK REG.

JUST THINK what those extra months of wear in AVONITE SOLES mean to a family budget. Children's shoes are outgrown before the soles wear out. For all the family, AVONITE SOLES are the only ones designed to wear as long as their uppers. That's why careful shoppers always look for the Solemark of Quality.

AVON SOLE COMPANY · · · AVON, MASSACHUSETTS
FOR FORTY YEARS SPECIALISTS IN FINE SOLE MATERIALS

not on all shoes . . . just the best ones

AVONITE SOLES—_dance on them_ . . . look like leather, feel like leather, give two, three times the wear of leather.

AVONITE SOLES—_work on them_ . . . waterproof—protect foot and general his. —keep shoes shapely, new looking.

AVONITE SOLES—_play on them_ . . . so flexible, comfortable, need no breaking in.

AVONITE SOLES are smart looking, firm, lightweight—do not mark floors.

AVONITE SOLES are approved for the Official Girl Scout Shoe.

GIRL SCOUT

1951

CAN YOU REMEMBER a time when shoe-sole companies put out ads? This one boasts that Avonite Soles give two to three times the wear of leather—now, that's the type of sole we'd shop for! It's no wonder they earned a seal of approval from the Girl Scouts.

"HAS ANYONE SEEN MY HOODED SWEATSHIRT?"

No family should be without one—or two or three or more! Mayo Spruce sweatshirts have wonderful up-and-down hoods. Fun! Look so smart. Go everywhere. Do anything—work, play, school, sports. Fleecy-warm cotton knit in scarlet, white, grey, olive, navy, powder blue. All sizes, men and women, $3.50. Children, sizes 4-8, $2.39; sizes 10-18, $2.79. Mayo Spruce, 5014 Empire State Building, N.Y. Products of Washington Mills Company, Winston-Salem, N.C.

MAYO **SPRUCE**

UNDERWEAR • SPORTSWEAR • SLEEPWEAR

You'll find your hooded sweatshirt by Mayo Spruce at the stores listed opposite.

CLOTHE THE WHOLE FAMILY in matching red hooded sweatshirts. Washington Mills developed polo shirts, sweatshirts, sports shirts and sleepwear in a variety of fabrics and colors. In 1954 it supplemented its well-known Mayo brand with a new line called Mayo Spruce.

TIGHT QUARTERS

Bev and I moved into our first home on Dec. 31, 1956. We found the place while visiting models in the Dunhurst Heights area of Wheeling, Illinois, the previous June. The subdivision was built in phases; ours went up in phase two and took about six months.

We paid $13,850 for a 1,000-square-foot, three-bedroom, one-bath ranch house, no money down. Payments were $82.75 a month, including taxes, and we had 30 years to pay.

We had three children when we moved in, and the house was quite comfortable. Over the years we added a detached garage, a screened-in porch and another four children, but Bev always managed to find a place to put things.

My son Gary wanted a train set, so we set out to accommodate him, building a platform on pulleys. Each time he wanted to use it, down came the 4-by-8-foot board, and back up it went when he was done.

It might sound impossible to live in a small house with a lot of people, but you can always find a way to make it work.

CHUCK MODROW · DIXON, IL

BUDGET CAMPING

My family did not have a lot of money when I was growing up in the '40s and '50s. Instead of going camping, we and all of our neighbors would get together to plan a campout in our backyards. There were no fences then, and all the yards ran into one another. We'd put out cots, small tents and sleeping bags. At night we would barbecue and eat in camp chairs. It was exciting to stay outside all night and look at the stars. In those days, you knew all of your neighbors within a four-block radius.

LINDA QUINLIVAN
VIA FACEBOOK

WITH FOUR YOU GET PLUMBING

BACK IN 1953, MY PARENTS, ELLEN AND STANLEY Peterson, lived on a farm near Wentworth, Wisconsin, with two daughters, Marie, 7, and Marlys, 16 months. The farmhouse lacked running water and had only an outhouse for certain needs. And Mom was pregnant.

When she had twins on Oct. 8, Dad vowed she would live in a house with running water and an indoor bathroom.

My sister Jean and I—those twins—were in incubators for some time. But when we were ready to go home, the family had already moved into a house in South Superior, Wisconsin.

We lived in the house for seven years, and I have so many memories of good times spent there.

JEANETTE EILEEN WEY · CEDAR RAPIDS, IA

Ellen and Stanley had no idea they were having twins. But the birth of daughters Jeanette and Jean was enough incentive to find a new home.

With four little girls—twins Jeanette and Jean on her lap and older sisters Marie (right) and Marlys—Ellen found indoor plumbing a godsend.

TWICE-TOLD NAMES

My twin sister and I were born on our mother's birthday in 1952. Our parents, Bob and Alice, named us after their mothers: I was called Raelene after our dad's mother, Rachel, and my sister Ellene was named in honor of our mom's mother, Ellen. Being named for our grandmothers makes us feel very special and unique.

RAELENE MAESTAS
LAKEWOOD, CA

MYSTERIOUS ELIXIR

In the early 1950s, our family lived with my grandmother and my grandfather, whom I called Tutt. Whenever Tutt got on the phone to order provisions from the local stores, my siblings and I pestered him to get us some Smith Bros. cherry cough drops. His answer was always the same: "I wouldn't give you snow water!"

I soon began to suspect that snow water must be really special. So one night I snuck into the pantry and looked high and low for it. I climbed a couple of shelves, to no avail. When I turned to leave, Tutt was waiting.

"What are you looking for?" he asked. I was afraid that I was in for it!

"Snow water," I said.

Tutt busted out laughing.

I escaped punishment but was still disappointed to learn that snow water was literally just melted snow.

R.G. AYERS
WILMERDING, PA

IT'S A FAMILY AFFAIR

My senior prom was set for June 1959. When I didn't get an invitation from the boy I hoped would ask me, I decided not to go. Then my cousin Barney, a year and a half younger than me but not from my school, said he'd take me, and I agreed. I borrowed a dress from Barney's sister Jean. My father drove us, and we went out for Chinese food afterward. Pretty tame compared to some proms, but a fun time thanks to the love and attention of my family.

MARY MARZANO · NORTH BELLMORE, NY

TWIN SETS

As if she wasn't busy enough as the mother of twins, Billie White also made all of Bobbie's and Becky's clothes, writes **BOBBIE DAVENPORT** of Huntsville, Alabama. Here they are in 1958, dressed up to join their father for lunch at the Officers Club in Camp Blanding, Starke, Florida.

DENVER 1952

In her cozy hooded coat, 5-year-old **JULIE NATALE**, now of Centennial, Colorado, helps her 2-year-old brother Kim navigate the grass on his scooter.

WAKE UP, SLEEPYHEAD

Dressed as their hero Hopalong Cassidy, it's no wonder brothers **KENNETH** and **LON CARNLEY** of Maiden, North Carolina, wore such big grins for the camera in 1951. "My brother was two years older and a sleepyhead," says Kenneth. "But I woke up early and went to the living room to find out what Santa had left. I was so excited, I woke Lon up and told him everything we had received."

HERE'S A WINNING FRAME

"My grandmother Yvonne Ostrander (center) and her sister Alice (right of center) bowled in a league for over 30 years," **BEVERLY CARUSONE** says. "They loved bowling and traveled all over the East Coast for tournaments."

SNOW SMILES

STEVE ABARTA of Simi Valley, California, was 13 when he tossed these snowballs at the camera with his mom, Betty, and brother Ron, 10, right. "We didn't see snow often in our part of the state," he writes. "So the trip to the mountains near Los Angeles in January 1955 was a real treat."

A Loving Hand Across the Cultural Fence

Two women bond in the melting pot of Hazel Park.

My mother, Ruby Chen, left Shanghai, China, in 1946 to be with her husband, Lionel Young, who was already in Detroit, Michigan. They first tried to buy a home in a certain neighborhood, but the residents promised to throw stones at them if they did. So they settled on a house in Hazel Park, a small city about 10 miles from Detroit.

Hazel Park was diverse in the 1950s. Our neighbors were Greeks, Italians, Poles, and families from Kentucky and Tennessee, who had come north to work in the automotive factories. My best friend, Marie Sirhan, was Syrian. My sister, my two brothers and I were the only children of Asian descent at our school, but I don't ever recall being made to feel that I was an outsider. In Hazel Park, there were no insiders or outsiders.

My mother had a difficult time adjusting to her new life. There were no telephone lines to China, and of course, no such things as email or Skype. The mail was slow. She had come from a very wealthy family in Shanghai and was used to having servants. Suddenly, she was hanging up her children's diapers in the snow!

Then she met our neighbor, Edith Mancini. They were about the same age but had little else in common.

My mother was a college graduate who taught accounting at the university level. She married my father when she was 26. Mrs. Mancini had an eighth-grade education, married at 17 and had eight children. Yet the two women became friends when Mrs. Mancini took my mother under her wing.

In the early 1950s, my mother had four kids under the age of 6. I'm sure she just got overwhelmed at times. She'd go over to the Mancinis' house and sit as Edith was doing her chores. It calmed my mother down.

When we moved to Seattle, we lost touch with the Mancinis. But after my father died in 1999, we re-established contact with Mrs. Mancini. Then, when my mother died in 2002, Mrs. Mancini became my dear friend. She is like another mother to me.

Edith Mancini represents the kind people of Hazel Park. They didn't have much money, but they were rich in love and hospitality. I am grateful to have grown up in such a place, among such good people.

EILEEN YOUNG · SEATTLE, WA

Ruby missed her life in China after she married Lionel and moved to Michigan in 1946. But friendship with neighbor Edith Mancini eased her homesickness.

Taking in the Sights

This is me with my mom (left) and her friend on top of Rockefeller Center in 1958, with a stunning view of Central Park and New York City as background. Mom is holding my little red purse, which matched my dress. At age 2, I was feeling really fabulous.

SUZY MOFFITT

ALL SMILES, these two were certainly happy to tie the knot in August 1959. With new love and a time of prosperity in America, the sky was the limit for newlyweds.

TRUE LOVE

"Come on snake, let's rattle!"
started many a romance in the
1950s as guys asked girls to dance.

Darling Art

Where have all the years gone? I can remember when you first came into my life, back in 1951! The first time you gave me and my boyfriend a ride home from a 5-cent dance. A few days later, you stopped in to the five-and-ten where I worked to buy a handkerchief. The next day, you came in to buy six screws. Then, a couple of days later, you called for a date. I had to turn you down. I remember telling you, "You have to call earlier," and you did.

We went to the early show—then up to the Friday-night dance. You held me so close when we danced, I could hardly breathe. Saturday, you called me again to hang out that night. After the movie, we parked in front of my house to "talk," and you kissed me! I was still in high school, and you were going to college. We met in the afternoons, and you became my only date.

After we dated for two weeks, you joined the Air Force. Before Christmas in 1951, you left to take your physical— thinking you would be back home for the holidays. But you were sent to Lackland Air Force Base in Texas. That was the last time we saw each other until May 1952.

You were writing me almost every day. From that day on, I never had a date with another boy. I knew I was "in love" with and very loved by you. You came home on leave in May—just as I was getting ready to graduate. We spent almost all of the nine days together. Little did I know, you had a diamond engagement ring in your pocket. On your last night home, you asked me, and I said yes! You gave me the reason to have the wedding I wanted. I made my white satin wedding gown with a long train and lots of lace. The invitations were mailed, and you got home two weeks before our big day.

When I walked down the aisle and saw you waiting, it was the happiest, most important day of my life. We honeymooned at a cute little cottage on a lake in northern Wisconsin. It didn't matter what we did in those days; we just wanted to hold on to each other.

You took my heart and held it tightly, and when I was ready, you gave me your heart. Even to this day, my darling, when you walk into a room, my heart beats a little faster.

Love forever,
Joan

JOAN DORN · BUFFALO, MN

Gerald earned his sergeant's stripes while serving in the Army during the Cold War.

Lois' charm was simply irresistible.

BLUE SKIES AHEAD

Chalk it up to her big smile and his stripes.

CALL IT CHANCE; CALL it divine providence. Our first meeting occurred in 1950 on Fourth Street in Huntingburg, Indiana, while I was visiting one of my sisters. I was 15. Two houses down, I noticed a man selling melons from a truck. So I walked over, and there stood a beautiful girl near the truck. I said hello and she smiled back, but that was about it. At the time, I was too shy to say any more.

Fast-forward five years and I was home on furlough proudly displaying my newly earned sergeant's stripes. My brother and I were walking east on Main Street when we passed a young woman walking toward us. I should have recognized that infectious smile, but I didn't. I felt my heart stop and stammered to my brother, "Who's that?"

"I thought you knew," he said. "That's Lois King, Bert King's daughter. He's chief of police here."

I vaguely remembered that Bert had a daughter and that they lived next door to my sister on Fourth Street. Then it hit me like a cannonball. This Lois was the girl with the million-dollar smile who'd left me speechless years ago. Funny what time can do to a person. To put it mildly, we had both changed.

I had to return to Ladd AFB near Fairbanks, Alaska, in a few days.

When I learned Lois was still in high school, in the same grade as my "baby" sister, we began writing to each other. I'll declare, you could almost see the blue smoke seeping from those letters.

We were married six months after my discharge.

I'm now in my 80s, and Lois and I've been married for more than 60 years. We have three girls and four boys. Two are preachers, one a mortician. To put it another way: Two to marry 'em, one to bury 'em.

People told us that we were too young and that we'd never stay together. But here we are propping each other up and reminding ourselves: "Old age is not for sissies."

GERALD MULLEN
LEETONIA, OH

Speaking from the Heart

With a few choice words, a young GI found lifelong happiness.

The year was 1952—one of the best of my life. That was the year I fell in love with Hanako Yamakita. I was barely 18 and on my first tour of duty with the Air Force in Japan. She worked in the PX as a seamstress. I worked at finding ways to see her: I quickly developed a habit of losing buttons from my uniform. Sometimes I needed stripes sewn onto my jacket. I saw my Hanako as much as I possibly could.

One day, she insisted that we travel from Johnson Air Base at Nishi-Tokorozawa to Gifu-ken, her hometown, so I could meet her parents. In keeping with Japanese tradition, I would ask for her hand in marriage.

Panic set in when I was greeted by 16 awed, silent faces. Hanako's relatives were kneeling on a straw mat spread over a well-scrubbed wooden floor in a large, airy room. They looked puzzled, even stoic, but polite.

I recalled the few words of Japanese that Hanako had taught me to say. "*Konnichiwa, minaasan* (Good evening, everyone)," I said. "*Watashi wa Nikorasu to moushimasu* (I am Nicholas)."

Smiles spread around the room. Hanako beamed. Encouraged, I followed up with "*Ogenki desu ka? (How are you?)*"

I cannot recall how much hot sake we consumed over the next two days, but Hanako later told me that I had been unanimously welcomed into the Yamakita clan. Before our surprise visit to the village, she'd made no attempt to tell her family about her surprise. They had never met an American before. What's more, they'd never met a black American or even seen one, except maybe in a magazine. They concluded that Americans weren't so bad after all, Hanako said.

Hanako and I shared 56 years together and raised three children. I lost my Hanako on July 24, 2008, one day after my 74th birthday.

JOHN PAUL NICHOLAS
RANCHO CORDOVA, CA

The couple pose together at top. Hanako wears her kimono (inset) outside the couple's first home in Nishi-Tokorozawa, Japan, early in their marriage. Years later, she wore the ceremonial wedding gown (bottom) during a visit to her family.

Wally and Donna Medin are pictured here with Linda, their flower girl, at Bethlehem Baptist Church on Nov. 5, 1954.

LETTERS TO KOREA

MY HUSBAND, WALLACE, AND I WOULD have never met if he hadn't been drafted into the Army for the Korean War. He and other men from Minnesota were ordered to meet at the Minneapolis Armory on the day after Thanksgiving in 1951. My boyfriend, George, was also in that group, and he and Wally became good friends. When their leave ended, George's plans changed, but Wally was sent to Korea. The boys wanted to keep in touch, but George didn't like to write, so I wrote to Wally for him.

George proposed soon after he was discharged, but it was a rocky romance, and I gave him his ring back after two and a half years. I wrote Wally to tell him the news and asked if I should still write him. He said yes. Our letters were friendly: "Dear Wally—your friend, Donna" and so on. He wrote back and asked if he could call me for a date when he was discharged, and I said yes.

It was a Thursday night in October 1953 when his call came. I was at Bethlehem Baptist Church in Minneapolis for choir practice. My mother told me he had called, so I went right home. Wally and I went roller-skating and had a good time.

My family and friends liked Wally right away. In March 1954, Wally asked me if I would like to get married. I told him I would have to pray about it for a week. When he came to the door of our home the next Friday night, Judy, my 13-year-old sister, got to the door first and said, "She's going to say yes!" And of course, I did!

Our wedding was at Bethlehem Baptist Church on a chilly Friday night, Nov. 5, 1954, and we honeymooned one week. We were blessed with three dear children after eight years of marriage—Debbie, Diane and Danny. We are now in our 80s and have been married more than 60 years. Wally often says, "We never would have met under ordinary circumstances, but God had it planned all along."

DONNA MEDIN · GREENDALE, WI

'50s DATING FOR DUMMIES

The 1950s ushered in a new age of dating as the first baby boomers—granted more freedom than any previous generation—hit their teen years.

....

Back then, dating had its own set of social rituals, including many that seem hopelessly quaint by today's standards. Here's a look back at some do's and don'ts that show why spending a Saturday night with your sweetheart during the Eisenhower era was the cat's meow.

....

DATING ETIQUETTE FOR GIRLS:

- Only floozies ask guys out.

- When someone asks you out, it's polite to give an immediate answer.

- Never break a date without providing a valid reason.

- There's no such thing as fashionably late; be ready when your date arrives.

- It's only proper to introduce your date to your parents.

- Don't apply makeup in public (please see the first point).

- At a restaurant, it's ladylike to tell a date what you want for dinner, so he can order for you.

- Don't humiliate guys by trying to pay for a date.

DATING ETIQUETTE FOR GUYS:

- Dates aren't like cramming for exams; don't wait until the last minute to ask a girl out.

- It's poor form to honk the car horn to announce your arrival; call for her at the door.

- Ask her parents when they want her back home—and make sure that your watch works.

- It's only polite to help her don her coat.

- Real gentlemen open car doors for girls—or any door, for that matter.

- It's chivalrous to walk between her and the curb.

- Bring enough money along.

- There's no kissing on the first date.

- On prom night, don't leave the corsage in the fridge.

LIKE MOTHER, LIKE DAUGHTER

In the summer of 1951, a coed friend of mine from Washburn University in Topeka, Kansas, asked to set me up on a blind double date with a friend of hers who had just broken up with a longtime boyfriend. I said OK, so the date was on for that coming Saturday. My friend, her date and I arrived at precisely the given hour.

I went to the door and rang the bell. The most beautiful girl answered. "I'm Jack," I said. "Are you ready to go?"

She responded, "My daughter will be down in just a few minutes."

I nearly collapsed with embarrassment. I later learned that my date's mother was elated; her father, maybe not so much. Either way, they would soon become my in-laws.

JACK BAINTER · OBERLIN, KS

STAGES OF ROMANCE

In 1953, my father, Kenneth Lundquist, was attending Georgia Tech in Atlanta. One afternoon, to escape boredom and the heat of the dorms, he wandered into an auditorium where the drama club was holding auditions for *Mister Roberts*. Dad just wanted to watch and cool off, but the play's director, Mary Nell, talked him into trying out. Much to his surprise, he ended up getting a part.

The next play the club put on was *Detective Story*, and he landed a part in it, too. Unlike *Mister Roberts*, *Detective Story* called for a few female roles. As there were few women at Georgia Tech at the time, the club recruited students from the drama club at nearby Oglethorpe University, including Sharon Moon, who won a role in the play.

Kenneth and Sharon continued their relationship after the play's run. Recently, Dad and Mom celebrated their 60th wedding anniversary. They have three children, five grandchildren and four great-grandchildren.

KIM LUNDQUIST ARNOLD
LAWRENCEVILLE, GA

Isabel and Enza have been together for more than 60 years.

"I thought since this was the second date, I should be able to have a kiss," Enza said.

Witness to a Kiss

Mother stood an arm's length away for Isabel's first one.

Enza and I met at a dance more than 60 years ago in the neighboring town of Ovid, Michigan. A couple of our mutual friends had introduced us. He was 19 at the time and I was 17.

On our second date we went to another dance. We ended the evening in my driveway, visiting in his car, a classy yellow Dodge convertible roadster with a black top and sharp air horns on the right front fender. That car was dreamy!

My mom, Magdalen Motz, quite watchful about how long I spent visiting in cars, would switch the porch light on and off to let me know it was time to end a date. So that night, when the lights started flickering, I went into the house and watched as Enza drove away.

Suddenly, he stopped the car, backed into the driveway, got out and came up the steps. I immediately opened the door to see what the problem was while my mother followed close behind me.

"I thought since this was the second date, I should be able to have a kiss," Enza said. And then he leaned in to kiss me, not knowing that my mom was right behind the open door.

So Mom witnessed my first kiss. She got quite a kick out of it, too.

Now, after more than 60 years of marriage, we still manage to kiss every day, but nothing is quite as memorable as that first one.

ISABEL VIGES · MIDLAND, MI

The Yankee and the Southern Belle

Jerry and his Alice share the same wedding-day smile some 60 years later. Only this time, there's less cake!

In June 1955, my good friend Larry, a Navy shipmate, asked me to attend church with him to meet his future bride, Alice.

As Alice approached us, I was completely mesmerized by her southern charm and natural beauty. What in the world could I do? I thought I had fallen in love with my friend's future wife. A few seconds later, though, another charming young lady appeared, and Larry introduced me to "his Alice." I was overcome with a blissful joy.

Shortly thereafter, Larry and "his Alice" departed, and I was alone with my Alice.

Before I knew it, I had blurted out, "You're going to think I am crazy when I tell you we are going to get married someday." Her instant reply was, "You are nuttier than a fruitcake; I don't date sailors or Yankees, so that will never happen!"

My plan was to start attending all the church events in which she was involved.

My future mother-in-law, an active member in church, got to know me and paid it forward by asking if I would like to have Sunday dinner with them. I jumped at the opportunity to develop a relationship with Alice.

Her father was recovering from a massive heart attack and invited me to visit him. We were both gin rummy and checkers players, and I developed a great friendship with him.

All these occurrences finally broke Alice's resistance, and we began to date. Just when things had begun to jell, I was sent on a six-month cruise to the North Atlantic. Absence proved to be what actually sealed the deal. We both missed each other so much that when I returned, I asked her to marry me.

We've celebrated more than 60 years of marriage together.

GERALD "JERRY" CALLAHAN
COLUMBIA, SC

CELEBRATIONS LASTED ALL DAY

MY HUSBAND, AL, AND I WERE MARRIED ON
Sept. 20, 1952, at 9 a.m. at St. Philip Church in East St. Louis, Illinois. In those days at our church, you had to be married before noon. After the ceremony we had breakfast at the Hitching Post in Belleville. My parents were divorced, so my mother paid for breakfast complete with a large layered wedding cake.

The rest of the afternoon was spent visiting St. Mary's Hospital, where our photographer's wife was recovering from an accident both of them had been in.

Then, along with our entire wedding party, we visited Al's grandpa, who couldn't attend the ceremony or the reception. He gave us a $100 bill—a lot of money in 1952.

Our reception was at 7 that evening above Edgemont Bowling Lanes. Receptions in the '50s were held wherever you could find room, and my father paid for ours. You climbed a flight of stairs to get to the banquet hall; it was a wonder the floor didn't collapse under the weight of so many people. The location turned out to be quite handy considering how many times my father went downstairs to the bowling alley to buy drinks and bring them back for my two new brothers-in-law.

We had no caterers, so our families prepared all the delicious food for us. We had a live band and gifts—no DJs or gift cards.

The reception ran until 2 a.m. and started up again that afternoon with family gathering to watch us open all the gifts.

We spent our honeymoon in the Lake of the Ozarks at Bagnell Dam in Missouri, where we took our grandchildren on vacation each year when they were young.

JEANNINE A. MEINEN · BELLEVILLE, IL

Toasting early, Jeannine and Al celebrated with one cake at breakfast, another in the evening.

FLEETING ATTRACTION

It was 1955. I was 21 and had just joined a Republican political club with one of my girlfriends. The monthly meetings were mostly social, with an occasional speaker. We played the jukebox and danced.

One member, Andy, was a dance instructor for the Arthur Murray Studios. He taught us all to dance the cha-cha. We girls liked to dance with Andy. He was a strong leader; we felt like Ginger Rogers dancing with Fred Astaire!

Andy asked me for a date, and we went to Jones Beach. When he took off his shirt, I could only think, *Wow! Great body!* When he took off his shoes, the thrill was gone. Andy's toenails were yellow and too long! Funny how first impressions can be lasting, even many years later!
JOAN RUSIELEWICZ · MERRICK, NY

ROSES ARE RED-HANDED

Because I lived in the far reaches of the country in the early '50s, Valentine's Day posed a problem for me: As a fifth-grader with no money or transportation, how was I to get my crush the valentine she deserved?

Luckily, my married sister, Jane, always made a trip home to bring my brothers and me a nice valentine. Admiring one year's card, I was struck with a brilliant idea.

After everyone had gone to bed on Valentine's eve, I found my card from Jane, carefully erased my name, and printed my beloved's name over the smudges. The next morning, I slipped the card into the box on the teacher's desk. The big moment arrived, and the teacher called the names one by one. I watched intently as my crush opened her card. I will never forget the look of bewilderment on her face when she read it. Her hand flew into the air. "Teacher," she asked, "why does mine say, Love, Jane & Richard?"
BILLY COTNER · JACKSON, TN

EXIT STAGE LEFT
Looking forward to their honeymoon in the Poconos in Pennsylvania, **JOHN MEYER**, now of Ocean View, Delaware, sweeps his new bride, Peggy, off her feet and out the door of the SSCC (Societa Santa Croce Camerina) Hall in Hackensack, New Jersey, where they held their wedding reception on Oct. 4, 1958.

DIAMOND ANNIVERSARY
My parents, Walter "Bud" and Joce Anna Govedich, were married July 20, 1957. They were high school sweethearts and are still going strong. They recently celebrated their diamond anniversary.
DEBBIE LANE • WILLOUGHBY HILLS, OH

> ❝
>
> *Laverne and I were married Sept. 5, 1954. I bought the embroidered Swiss eyelet for my wedding dress, and my mother made the dress and veil. My ancestors came from Switzerland, so the fabric was fitting.*
>
> **MARIANNE J. LEDERMAN**
> BRODHEAD, WI

CECILIA CROUL
PHILADELPHIA, PA
MARRIED: Sept. 2, 1950
MY DRESS: Satin and lace; peplum; satin-covered buttons; short train
MY VEIL: Juliette-style cap; fingertip-length veil

DOROTHY TUCKER BEHRENS
HARVARD, IL
MARRIED: Sept. 16, 1950
MY DRESS: Satin; lace neckline; a ruffled accent on the bodice
MY VEIL: Waist-length; lace trim

Bill and Kathleen stepped through the Citadel ring and into a long, beautiful life together at the spring hop in 1952.

The caller stopped the music and pointed to us. He wouldn't take no for an answer!

The Square Dance Chose Them

On an unusually warm evening for October, but not uncommon for Charleston, South Carolina, the nuns gave us students at the St. Francis Xavier School of Nursing a square dance. They invited the local cadets from the Citadel to join us.

I didn't know how to square-dance, so I clung to the wall, afraid to be noticed. A lack of knowledge didn't stop the other students. The music and laughter floated all around, tempting me.

There was a cadet hanging on to the opposite wall. The caller stopped the music and pointed to both of us. He wouldn't take no for an answer!

We joined a circle and soon got the hang of allemanding right and left. This sure was better than solitude.

I was having such a good time with this blue-eyed, blond, curly-headed cadet. It's hard to believe I almost missed my chance at meeting this wonderful man. His name was Bill, and he was from Atlantic City.

After months of dating, we went to the spring hop together. As we danced through a huge Citadel ring, Bill put a miniature ring on my finger. We were officially engaged.

We married on Jan. 9, 1953, after a two-year courtship. We've been together for more than 60 years, and we are blessed with five children and eight grandchildren.

KATHLEEN WOLFE HENNE
CAMP HILL, PA

THE JEWELRY BOX
THAT CHANGED EVERYTHING

IN OCTOBER 1955, I WAS TO BE
a bridesmaid in my sister's wedding.
She had set up a blind date for me with
Aurel, my brother-in-law's neighbor,
but I already had a date with a steady
boyfriend. I was as mad as a wet hen when
I had to cancel it. I didn't even like Aurel
when I met him, but I agreed to go out
the two additional nights he was in Iowa.

When he was getting
ready to return to Kansas,
he asked if I would write
to him. We wrote every
week from October 1955
to May 1956.

On Valentine's Day,
I received a jewelry box
from Aurel, marking
the turning point in our
relationship. I finally had
something tangible to
represent our love.

Aurel proposed to me
on a Saturday night while
we were sitting in his
1953 Ford. Miraculously,
in the time since our first
unimpressive date, he
had grown tremendously
attractive! Aurel's response
to my affirmative answer

was "Good! Let's go pick out the rings!"
The little jewelry store in town was still
open, and we did just that.

We spent Christmas in Kansas City with
the rest of his family. It was hugs and kisses
like I'd never experienced before! They
had been so sure Aurel was doomed to
be a permanent bachelor and were thrilled
to find out how wrong they were! We
married on April 28, 1957. And I still have
the jewelry box, now full of the treasures
from our life together.

JEANETTE MONTGOMERY
SABETHA, KS

Jeanette and Aurel Montgomery
after their beautiful spring
wedding on April 28, 1957.

Slow and Steady Wins the Race

Persistence helped overcome a bad first impression.

Maudie and I have been married for more than 50 years, but it most certainly was not love at first sight. We both grew up in Mobile, Alabama, and entered Murphy High School in 1953 as freshmen. Mobile had high school fraternities and sororities then and still does—social organizations, but unlike the ones in college. By the second semester of my sophomore year, I had joined a fraternity.

In civics class I sat by two sorority girls. The three of us talked so much during class that the teacher split us up. She moved me next to a girl named Maudie. The only thing I knew about Maudie was that she was best friends with the daughter of the prominent pastor at the largest Baptist church in Mobile. As far as I was concerned, that was all I needed to know about her. And Maudie knew all she wanted to know about me.

In our junior year, we were in the same bookkeeping class. I liked the class but I had trouble with some of the problems. I knew Maudie was smart, so I asked her for help. Without a word, she let me know she had no desire to help me. So I asked another classmate.

Then in our senior year, I started working in a grocery store. Maudie came in weekly with her mother and seemed to be a different person. We talked as I bagged the groceries and I realized that I had changed, too.

One night as I took the groceries out for her, I asked if she wanted to hang out and go for a ride when I got off work, but she said she had to drive her mother home. I felt rejected but found out later that she was hoping I would offer to pick her up after I was done with work.

Several days later I drove past her as she walked home from school and offered her a ride. She accepted and I quickly asked her for a date to a revival at our church—I'd picked the revival on purpose, thinking she'd be more likely to accept. And she did. We continued to date steadily until that prominent Baptist preacher married us on April 3, 1959.

JOHN DOUGLAS "DOUG" GREEN
BELLEVIEW, FL

Doug Green and Maudie Green—yes, that was her maiden name—found more to like about each other as time went by.

Without a word, she let me know she had no desire to help me.

Carolyn and Will lived for two years
(until their first child was on the way)
in this jadeite green home on wheels.

TINY, BUT NEARLY PERFECT

TINY! THERE WAS NO OTHER WORD FOR IT.
Our first home measured 8 feet by 20 feet—smaller
than our present living room—but it was perfect
for newlyweds.

We married in December 1956, a week after my
husband, Will, graduated from college. The next
week we moved from the Midwest to the snowy,
frigid state of New York so he could begin work.

We purchased a mobile home that only Will
had seen from his sister and brother-in-law, and
we had it transported to New York prior to our
arrival. No words can adequately describe my
initial shock at seeing the small space we would
call home for the next two years.

Yes, it was tiny, but the joy we shared in that
little space was huge. A thousand miles from
our families, we learned to lean on each other
and trust that we would be there for each other,
no matter what.

CAROLYN Y. RICKMAN · HILTON, NY

LOVE SONGS OF THE '50s

Whether we were making out or
making up, these are the ballads
that made us weak in the knees.

"Love Letters in the Sand"
Pat Boone

....

"Love Me Tender"
Elvis Presley

....

"Young Love"
Sonny James

....

"Love Is a Many-Splendored Thing"
The Four Aces

....

"All I Have to Do Is Dream"
The Everly Brothers

....

"Venus"
Frankie Avalon

....

"I Only Have Eyes for You"
The Flamingos

....

"Secret Love"
Doris Day

....

"On the Street Where You Live"
Vic Damone

....

"Since I Don't Have You"
The Skyliners

....

"Kisses Sweeter Than Wine"
Jimmie Rodgers

....

"Tonight You Belong to Me"
Patience and Prudence

MUSICOR

Vintage Ads

In the 1950s, advertisers used love to sell just as much as they do today, but the times have certainly changed.

Chocolate Cherries pick the finest!

Brach's Chocolate Cherries—thick bittersweet chocolate covers selected plump cherries centered in smooth, cordialled vanilla creme. Only the finest imported flavors are used in this fine Brach candy. 24 tempting pieces to the pound.

Brach's
MAKES THEM BETTER

1950

WHILE VALENTINE'S DAY ads get more outrageous each year, this one for chocolate cherries keeps it simple. And with a candy this luxe, who needs a gimmick?

What a Kiss I Got that night

My husband was frantic when he came home from work. He had forgotten that this was the night the boys were coming over for poker.

But I hadn't. There was plenty of cold Budweiser in the refrigerator to go along with my snacks.

When they'd gone, he said, "Even the ones who lost had a good time . . . thanks to the good things to eat, the Budweiser and your good memory."

(Actually, Budweiser reminded me, when I saw it at the store. When I see Budweiser, I think of hospitality . . . letting people know you think enough of them to serve the best.)

Budweiser
KING OF BEERS

ANHEUSER-BUSCH, INC.
ST. LOUIS • NEWARK • LOS ANGELES

"Where There's Life . . . There's Bud!"

MAY 1956

45

1956

BUDWEISER PORTRAYS a more sentimental time in beer advertising by celebrating romance. Today, its less people-centric ads focus on animals, like the iconic Clydesdales and croaking frog puppets.

Aren't today's people wonderful?

JUST being around them makes you feel good! They're so wonderful to look at—these slender, handsome, active men and women of today.

Their wholesome, up-to-date eating habits— their modern taste for lighter, less filling food— have a lot to do with it.

Today's Pepsi-Cola, reduced in calories, goes right along with this sensible trend in diet. Never heavy, never too sweet, Pepsi-Cola refreshes without filling.

Have a Pepsi—the modern, the *light* refreshment.

Pepsi-Cola
The *Light* refreshment

PEPSI-COLA PLAYS off the young and fit here, promoting its product as "the modern, the light refreshment." Get inspired by this vintage ad and create a fantastic menu for a picnic at the beach with your sweetie.

What started as a letter-filled long-distance relationship turned into more than 50 years of marriage.

AN AVID LETTER WRITER

I was 13 in 1955 and, back then, a big fan of teen magazines. They always included a section with the names and addresses of readers who wanted to become pen pals. I decided to write to a boy in Minnesota and was excited to receive a letter from him. Over the next couple of years we stayed in touch; he called me "L'il Sis."

After a while he told me about a girl named Jane whom he'd started dating. Soon Jane and I became pen pals. We wrote each other for about two years, and she invited me to visit her family after I graduated from high school. During my visit, I met Jane's brother, Lenny. It didn't take long for me to realize I was falling for him.

Jane married my pen pal in 1962, and they paired Lenny and me at the wedding. After a long-distance relationship of more than four years that included back-and-forth letter writing, we were married.

We celebrated our 50th wedding anniversary on Jan. 30, 2015, on the beach of Waikiki, Hawaii. We now have four beautiful children, a wonderful grandson and a fabulous life. When I mention our '50s teen magazine beginnings, I like to say my husband married his Annette and I married my Elvis!

JOAN SIBINSKI
COON RAPIDS, MN

News Traveled Fast

She was married in the same tiny house where she was born.

My fiance, Gary Evans, and I decided to get married on June 9, 1956, just after my high school graduation. We didn't have money for a formal wedding or a gown. I didn't expect those things because they weren't important to me. However, my dad, Kelly Sizemore, had other ideas.

He was a coal miner, and the company store sold merchandise that employees could put on credit. Dad took me shopping and I chose a simple dotted-swiss, street-length dress. I wore it with my graduation shoes and a hat with no veil. The dress was beautiful and I appreciated my dad for seeing to it that I had something so nice to wear for the wedding.

The ceremony took place in a small country church on Tams Mountain in West Virginia, a stone's throw from the house where I grew up. The building had been converted into a place of worship from a small two-room house where my parents had lived while our house was being built across the road. In fact, my sister Jean and I were born in that two-room house.

My cousin Louise and Gary's older brother Earl were our wedding attendants. Our preacher and friend, Okey Cox, performed the ceremony. We had no music; we sent out no invitations. Yet somehow that little building was full of family, friends and neighbors offering smiles and happy wishes for our union. I guess news travels fast in a small community.

FERN EVANS · BEAVER, WV

A simple ceremony, Fern and Gary's wedding may have been the only one ever performed at that church, Fern says.

Kathy (left) wears the gown her grandmother made for Joyce (above). Over the years, the lace has turned a creamier color than when first worn.

TWO DREAMS COME TRUE

WITH MY WEDDING fast approaching, I began putting serious thought into what I wanted for my gown. Even after looking at a number of *Brides* magazines, I was unable to find the perfect dress.

Remembering that my fiance's mom enjoyed sewing, I asked her if she would make my gown, provided I found her some patterns. She readily agreed. I'll never forget the special trips to fabric stores with my mom-to-be, who was filled with patience, to pick out the patterns and the materials for my dress.

After a time, everything fell into place, and I was ecstatic on the day of my last fitting. As I looked into the mirror with my mom-to-be at my side, I realized she had made my dreams come true. Not only was she giving me her son—she had also given me the perfect gown.

When my daughter, Kathy, was planning her wedding 29 years later, she said she wanted to wear my gown. We unwrapped it for the first time since 1959, and she loved it just as much as I did.

On Kathy's big day, I watched my mother-in-law as her granddaughter walked down the aisle in the same lace gown she had sewn all those years ago. I knew then that she realized how much she had given two women on their wedding days.

JOYCE GOODRICH
SAVANNAH, NY

Delaine and Donald Ewen on March 25, 1951, the day after their wedding.

Love Always Finds a Way

The year was 1950, and the Korean War was on. I didn't worry too much that my fiance, Don, would be drafted. He had flat feet and would, of course, be excused. But Uncle Sam was not interested in our love affair, only an induction date.

After Don's three months of basic training at Fort Riley, Kansas, his family and I thought he'd have the usual furlough before being shipped overseas. It was on that assumption I planned our wedding, 150 miles away, in my hometown. The church and pastor were confirmed, as well as the photographer, florist, baker, etc. Invitations were ordered and sent out. All was going well, until Don called, saying his

leave would be two weeks later. I notified everyone involved. Again, all going well, until another call from Don revealed that he wasn't getting a furlough at all.

The ladies of my church had scheduled a bridal shower for me, prior to my original wedding date. A harsh winter storm blew in, and getting out to attend my shower was looking impossible. Even the weather wasn't on my side! A neighbor pulled the only conveyance that could accommodate my mother and me—a manure spreader. Sitting wrapped in rugs and blankets, we were driven 3 miles to the main highway, where we met a friend who took us to the shower site.

After our initial wedding plans fell through, my dear in-laws offered to drive me to Fort Riley so Don and I could get married there. In our eagerness, we hadn't realized it was Good Friday. The courthouse was closed.

Undaunted, we spent all night driving through stormy winter weather back to Minneapolis, where we had a license. We arrived at Don's parents' house at 6 a.m. on Saturday. His mother made us waffles, while I called the pastor. An impromptu wedding was set for noon.

I shook out my dress from its traveling box, did what I could with my hair, and walked down the aisle to meet my soldier husband. No weather or war could keep me from marrying my guy!

DELAINE EWEN • BLOOMINGTON, MN

A neighbor pulled the only conveyance that could accommodate my mother and me—a manure spreader.

Proposal, Then Prom

We went steady for a year before Ed asked me to marry him at my house just before we attended the Niles McKinley High School prom on May 23, 1952. We were married a year later.

JOHANNA YOUNG · NILES, OH

HAPPY DAYS and good times galore are the order of the day for these students from Long Beach Polytechnic High as they pile into their convertibles at Merle's Drive-In restaurant in Long Beach, California.

FADS, FASHION AND FUN

A new style swept the country, from the kitchen table to local hangouts, and it was clearly 1950s.

THE WISDOM OF BROWNIE WISE

Her most effective sales pitch was a literal pitch, tossing a covered bowl of juice across the room.

SHE WAS A SOUTHERN BELLE WITH a gift for sales. Divorced and with a son to support, Brownie Wise was selling Stanley Home Products in suburban Detroit, Michigan, using Stanley's proven sales model, the home party. A top seller, Brownie had her eye on the executive suite, but the head of the company told her no woman would reach that level.

So she quit, and started selling Earl Tupper's products at home. Brownie moved to Florida, and was soon racking up more sales than anyone else. By 1951, Tupper wanted to know her secret. She replied with a bold idea: Sell Tupperware only through home parties. He agreed and made her general manager—and soon vice president—of the new division.

Under Brownie's tutelage, Tupperware sales reached $25 million by 1954, when Brownie was the first woman to appear on the cover of *Business Week*. She motivated her sales force with contests, giveaways and pep rallies.

In time, Tupper chafed at her fame, which he felt overshadowed his product. After a protracted battle of wills, Tupper fired Brownie in 1958. She would never regain her footing in business.

Daring displays of Tupperware prowess were key to Wise's theory that customers had to see and feel the product to love it.

Sales of a Lifetime

Here and there for 60 years: journeys with Tupperware.

My partnership with Tupperware started in the late 1950s, when I was a high school student and 4-H member in Irvington, Nebraska. I went with my mother to a Tupperware party at a neighbor's house. My mother and three of her friends pooled their money to buy a set of square containers that would fit their husbands' sandwiches.

I decided that day that I wanted to host my own party. Even though I was still in school, I had experience doing public demonstrations from my 4-H shows and a love for the kitchen. I threw a lot of Tupperware parties for my dealer.

When I got married and had a baby, I became a dealer. After the birth of my third daughter I found myself the sole supporter of my family. I was promoted to Tupperware manager and qualified for the car program, which was very helpful financially.

A few years passed and I married again. Otto, my husband, dreamed of owning his own plane, and thanks to my Tupperware sales, we bought a four-passenger Cessna 182. He would fly me to my out-of-town Tupperware parties.

On Thanksgiving Day in 1975, we were at Disney World when I got a call that Tupperware had a distributorship available in Sioux Falls, South Dakota. Two months later, we moved our family of seven to a farm outside the city. A barn with a kitchen stall became our warehouse.

Within a few months, I'd turned the kitchen stall into the set for *Down Home*

Delights with Linda, a cooking show I created for local TV. Microwave cooking was still in its infancy at the time, so when Tupperware came out with a line of products designed for stack cooking in the microwave, I arranged to do demonstrations of the technique at grocery and appliance stores and other Tupperware distributor locations across the country.

One day in 1996, I was very surprised when the company president asked me to go to India as one of three people selected to introduce Tupperware home sales in developing markets. (The others went to China and Russia, but those divisions never took off and soon closed.) I left South Dakota thinking I'd be in India for a few weeks, but I stayed there almost a year, establishing teams in two cities.

At 75, I have 60 years of dedication to Tupperware. In most Augusts, I have my usual booth selling Tupperware at the fair in Parker, South Dakota. I'm thankful for my success—they wouldn't have kept me around for this long if I hadn't been successful!

LINDA HAGEDORN · TEA, SD

If we build the people, they'll build the business.

BROWNIE WISE

A WOMAN could earn up to $100 a week as a Tupperware dealer—far more than she could make in a traditional job, such as teacher, nurse or office secretary.

TUPPERWARE ADS: BROWNIE WISE PAPERS, ARCHIVES CENTER, NATIONAL MUSEUM OF AMERICAN HISTORY, SMITHSONIAN INSTITUTION

ware Seal... that makes the "difference!"

SEALING

LOCKS OUT moisture...dryness

Handy new utility tab is to hang Seals out of the way when not in use. Seal Rack for holding Seals is shown on page 19.

Food editors and home economists praise kitchen-tested Tupperware. It bears the Good Housekeeping and Parents' Magazine Seals.

IF PRODUCT OR PERFORMANCE DEFECTIVE
Good Housekeeping
GUARANTEES
REPLACEMENT OR REFUND TO CONSUMER

COMMENDED by **PARENTS'** MAGAZINE AS ADVERTISED THEREIN

See page 46 for information on Tupperware care.

hen Seal aps into ace, lift tab ghtly and ess center Seal to ex- air.

TO OPEN

1
Hold container in place and peel Seal back by pulling tab and twisting wrist.

5

2
Hold container down 'til Seal is completely off. Wash with swish of suds.

Your Guarantee of Quality...
Only top quality material goes in-to Tupperware. Vigilant quality control makes it the finest plastic housewares, guaranteed against defects in workmanship and materials.

IT WASN'T A BURP, exactly—more like a *whoosh*. But the homey term recalled essential duties of motherhood. Bowl covers, based on an inverted paint-can lid, formed the Tupperware Seal. The invention coincided with growing interest in food care and hygiene, and was a better alternative to aluminum foil for storage in the refrigerator.

1950

CAN YOU imagine life before front-loading dishwashers like this one? The original automatic dishwasher was a wooden wheel laid flat inside a copper boiler.

Hotpoint's Great Front

Hotpoint Automatic Electric Dishwasher Sink WITH AMAZING NEW "WONDERFLO" FAUCET

● Among the 1950 Hotpoint combinations featuring the dishwasher is the beau-tiful new Dishwasher Sink, finished in white porcelain enamel—styled and stream-lined for Hotpoint's matched appliance line. This model gives you the sensa-tional new "Wonderflo" Faucet which governs the force and temperature of water with a single, simple control. Now you can change the volume of water coming from the tap, to suit your requirements, without changing the temperature!

Look To Hotpoint For The Finest—FIRST!

RANGES · REFRIGERATORS · DISHWASHERS · DISPOSALLS® · WATER HEATERS · FOOD

The Convenient Kitchen

Advertisers offered '50s housewives laborsaving appliances and quick and easy foods.

Can you identify this person? She's wearing a dress, ruffled apron, heels and a cheerful smile. She's tidied the house, fixed a home-cooked meal, freshened up and seated her children at the table, and now she awaits the return of her hardworking husband from a long day at the office.

She's the ideal housewife of the 1950s—as imagined by the media at the time. She's also known by *Time* magazine as "the keeper of the suburban dream." The '50s homemaker had a lot on her plate,

and appliance and food manufacturers were happy to lighten her load.

APPLIANCES APLENTY

From toasters to stand mixers to ranges, electric appliances promised convenience, efficiency and styling. Magazine ads touted the benefits of kitchen items that, as one cookware manufacturer assured, would establish a woman's "reputation as a fine cook and clever hostess."

International Harvester refrigerators were "femineered," offering "scores of

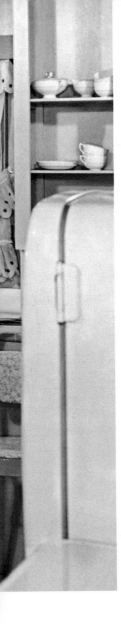

The modern kitchen of the 1950s was a clear step up in design and functionality.

chore-saving, women-approved features." General Electric automatic dishwashers promised to save "over 200 hours of work a year." The Presto electric pressure cooker assured busy cooks they could fix Sunday menus any day of the week, because the time-saving appliance did "an hour's cooking in 20 minutes!"

"Automatically" was the word of the day. Sunbeam's waffle iron made "four good-sized waffles at one time… automatically!" Servel offered "the world's only refrigerator that makes a continuous supply of ice cubes without trays automatically!" And West Bend's Flavo-Matic electric percolator was "nearly magic the way it automatically brews the best tasting coffee ever!"

THE NEW "FAST FOOD"

The '50s cook was encouraged to trim time from meal preparation with convenience foods, "ready mixes," canned goods and frozen foods. Advertisers emphasized the ease of preparation— not always flavor. Among the new "in a jiffy" food items introduced during this decade were Mrs. Paul's fish sticks, Lipton dehydrated onion soup mix, Cheez Whiz, Tang breakfast drink, Duncan Hines cake mixes and Rice-A-Roni.

Print and broadcast advertising boosted items launched years earlier, such as Campbell's condensed soups. Cream soups were a mainstay of such dinner delights as tuna noodle casserole, meat loaf "frosted" with mashed potatoes and green bean casserole, which was created in 1955 and remains popular today.

Other quick and easy recipes in ads included Fiesta Peach Spam Bake, using Spam canned meat and canned peaches; Pie Plate Salad, blending Veg-All canned mixed vegetables with lemon gelatin; and Tuna-Rice au Gratin, with Minute Rice and Carnation evaporated milk.

Even better than canned foods, frozen foods—from juices to vegetables to fish—were promoted as the ultimate in convenience. In 1954, as television moved into more American homes, Swanson TV dinners were introduced. Ads proclaimed: "No work before…no dishes after! But what a meal!" Indeed, the partitioned aluminum trays with meat, potato and vegetables were ready in a snap.

HOMEMADE WITH LOVE

Though ads lauded shortcut suppers, many home cooks continued to prepare simple meals from scratch. *Betty Crocker's Picture Cookbook* from 1950 includes pot roast, savory stew, fried chicken and plenty of other traditional fare. And any child of the '50s probably remembers the heavenly aroma of homemade cakes and cookies in the kitchen.

Sunday dinner, usually served around midday or after church, was sacred in many homes. Usually a meat-and-potatoes affair, it offered families an opportunity to sit around the table and connect. Children were expected to be neatly dressed and to help clean up. And rarely, if ever, were preferences indulged. Clean plates were expected, while moms across the country perfected their guilt-inducing "There are starving children in China" speech.

American takes on foreign cuisine emerged. Soldiers returning from faraway lands developed new tastes for ethnic foods, so suburban housewives obliged with watered-down versions of chop suey, French pilaf, Spanish rice, curried lamb and Polynesian fare, spurring an interest in canned pineapple (pineapple upside-down cake, anyone?) and exciting presentation techniques like flambe.

While some will recall the decade for onion soup dip and weird molded salads, others will remember the care of home cooks. But there's one thing everyone can agree on: Food was a fun part of the '50s.

APPLIANCES
Vintage Ads

Getting the best for your kitchen in the 1950s involved some choices in color coordination.

Exciting new col
Frigidaire makes yo

Make this advertisement your buying guide. Take it to your Frigidaire Dealer's today and ask him to tell you all the advantages of the refrigerator, upright food freezer, or electric range that catches

The striking new Cycla-matic Frigidaire offers complete Self-Service !

Behind this colorful new beauty is a new concept of food-keeping to make your life easier. Scores of startling new Self-Service features literally hand you food . . . save you countless steps and motions every day. You'll find Quickube Ice Trays, full-width Roll-to-You Shelves, and automatic removal of frost and defrost water. Unique Pantry-Doors have new egg servers, special compartments for butter and cheese, even handy server trays. And there's a complete range of sizes all the way up to 15 cubic feet.

New Frigidaire Electric Ranges are easiest of all to use

The colorful Frigidaire Electric Ranges, too, are designed t and trouble . . . to give you the easiest, most accurate top-a and automatic baking and roasting known. There's a offering 7 ways to cook without an extra pot, pan or sk Oven model gives you one or two ovens in a jiffy. The sen 30's—only thirty inches wide—fit big range quality and of the smallest kitchen. And there are many more models to

New G-E Wall Refrigerator-Freezer puts all foods at your eye level!

This big, new 11-cubic-foot General Electric Wall Refrigerator-Freezer *is the most convenient of all refrigerators,* because it puts all foods within easy reach.

You just reach right out and pick the foods you want. There's no need to bend or stoop for foods because everything is at eye level and can be seen at a glance. Even in the true, zero-degree freezer, shelves are easily accessible.

Hangs on your wall like a picture! It's so easy to install! There's little or no remodeling neces-

sary. Cabinet is hung on a sturdy "picture hook" mounting bracket which is fastened securely to the wall. Can be hung at any height to suit yourself.

See this luxurious new General Electric Wall Refrigerator-Freezer at your General Electric dealer's. Ask about the easy terms and generous trade-in allowance most General Electric dealers are offering. Household Refrigerator Department, General Electric Company, Appliance Park, Louisville 1, Kentucky.

Let your General Electric dealer *show you how easily you can transform your kitchen with little or no remodeling.* The simple addition of General Electric's magnificent Wall Refrigerator will add new beauty, new freshness and a new personality to your kitchen. Above at right the old cabinets and refrigerator have been taken out. On the wall—at eye level—is the new G-E Wall Refrigerator-Freezer. Underneath is a charming and practical desk unit.

BEFORE   AFTER

New G-E Wall Refrigerator comes in these Mix-or-Match colors: Canary Yellow, Turquoise Green, Petal Pink, Cadet Blue, Woodtone Brown—or White.

So much room for all your foods

1. 11 cubic feet of space. 2. Big automatic-defrost refrigerator section. 3. Permanent General Electric Alnico Magnetic Doors provide sure seal . . . close silently. 4. Separate vegetable and fruit compartments. 5. Adjustable door shelves for small jars and cans. 6. 2-cubic-foot

true zero-degree food freezer holds up to 70 pounds or 83 packages. 7. New-style Mini-Cube® ice trays. 8. Dependable and whisper-quiet sealed-in General Electric refrigeration system. 9. Complete unit is 64 inches long, 39½ inches high, 17¾ inches deep.

Progress Is Our Most Important Product
GENERAL ⊛ ELECTRIC

MAJOR APPLIANCE manufacturer General Electric launched a number of industry firsts in the mid-'50s while advertising its products' modern appeal. The GE Wonder Kitchen featured a built-in range, dishwasher, disposal, and washer and dryer under a single countertop. The sleek wall-mounted side-by-side refrigerator-freezer, left, has the look of kitchen cabinetry.

to glorify your kitchen!

righter—your daily chores lighter!

New Upright Food Freezer Color-Styled, too!

Every Frigidaire refrigerator and range is available in matching shades of green or yellow, in addition to snowy white—even the new upright Food Freezer is colorful and glamorous. Never before such a combination of styling and conveniences . . . never before such a choice of models to fit every need! See these new products Arthur Godfrey recommends on TV and radio. Look for your Frigidaire Dealer's name in your phone book under "Electrical Appliances." Or write Frigidaire, Dept. 2239, Dayton 1, Ohio. In Canada, To   ario.

Millions live better with

Frigidaire Appliances

Built and backed by General Motors

1954

AS BRIGHT shades debuted in 1950s kitchens, cooks could choose appliances in hues of yellow, pink, blue or copper for the family gathering spot.

APPLIANCES GET A PRETTY PALETTE

General Electric introduced mix-and-match colors for appliances in 1955.

....

CANARY YELLOW

PETAL PINK

TURQUOISE GREEN

CADET BLUE

WOODTONE BROWN

WALL-HUNG WONDER

When **STEPHEN BRITTAIN** bought his Fort Myers, Florida, home, he gained a General Electric Wall Refrigerator-Freezer built in 1955—its turquoise finish matching the sink, cabinets and range. The unit had not operated in 31 years. Fortunately, a friend and refrigeration expert persuaded Stephen to let him try repairing it. With a new fan motor and starting relay, the unit fired up. "The refrigerator still runs quietly on the original Freon," Stephen says. "It's a great novelty."

WHEN COLOR WAS QUEEN

Two pale turquoise General Electric wall ovens from 1952 grace the Charlottesville, Virginia, home that **KAREN** and **SCOTT KNIERIM** purchased in 1983. "I've always loved their color," Karen says. "In fact, we made over the whole kitchen to match." Scott handled it all, painting the cabinets a deep turquoise, and spraying the dishwasher and refrigerator with a matching shade of auto-body paint.

◆◆◆

TAG-SALE TREASURE

My hairdresser, Terry, works out of her home. Being a close friend, I looked around before my appointment to see what was new. My jaw dropped when I spotted this old refrigerator. Terry had gone to a late friend's estate sale and bought the retro work of art she had admired from afar. She paid $90 (getting a chair as part of the deal, too). It works like a charm.

DENISE DRAGOVICH
MOUNT VERNON, WA

Lean, Green Cooking Machine

We bought our first home by flashlight, not knowing we had a green jewel in the kitchen. Our first question: How much for the house? Our second question: Do the appliances go with it? My pulse quickened when the Realtor said yes.

"Didn't they ever use it?" I asked about the stove.

"Not really," she said.

Shaking my head, I muttered, "Well, it's going to get used now!" Saying a prayer, I turned knobs and waited for all of 10 seconds before the element coils turned bright orange. There was still some life in the old Frigidaire.

From then on, winter meant bread baking for the green stove and me, followed by pie and cookie making. Each summer produced 100 to 125 canning jars steaming with hot fruit. Still, the old green stove rattled on, heating those jars until they were processed, sealed and lined up on the counter.

When the workhorse finally started to tire, she needed a chair propped in front of her larger oven door to keep it closed. Eventually, a burner sizzled and burned out. And at last, the oven element was cold to the touch. The electrician shook his head and said, "Sorry." My heart thumped with panic.

But then he said, "I have a picture to show you." The next day, a white Monarch stove arrived, which we set up next to our green Frigidaire. Our new 1950s workhorse, which was molded in Wisconsin by the Malleable Iron Range Co., can cook, and it can do so almost as fast as its predecessor!

CHER L. TOM · PALISADE, CO

Cher's stoves earn their keep in her always-cooking Colorado kitchen.

ADVENT OF TV DINNER SOLVED MANY PROBLEMS

Swanson devised a three-compartment aluminum tray and filled the first ones with turkey dinners—turkey and cornbread stuffing with gravy, sweet potatoes and peas.

The resulting "heat and serve" dinner was considered somewhat risky, so only 5,000 were ordered. In 1955, the first year of national distribution, Swanson sold 10 million of the dinners.

The item was a time-saver for millions of women who continued to work outside the home in jobs they'd started during a manpower shortage in World War II. It also allowed families to enjoy a hot meal with minimal preparation while watching television.

Today the concept is such a part of Americana that an original TV dinner package is part of the Smithsonian Institution collection.

WHEN THE SWANSON TV DINNER appeared in 1954, it was the solution to several different situations.

After Thanksgiving 1953, Swanson had a surplus of turkeys—520,000 pounds to be exact—and limited warehouse space for the birds. To keep them cold, they were kept in refrigerated railroad cars traveling from coast to coast.

At the time, Gerry Thomas was the company's vice president of marketing. He saw a single-compartment tray being tested by an airline to serve meals on international flights and asked for a sample tray.

PRICES CIRCA 1950

Gas range	$ 99.95
Box of soap flakes	.29
16 rolls of colored toilet paper	$ 1.15
4 lbs. of navy beans	.22
Tin of Planters peanuts	.31
1 lb. of graham crackers	.29
3 boxes of Jell-O	.23

WHAT A TREAT!

I recall eating TV dinners in front of our black-and-white television in the '50s. My mother would spread newspapers out on the floor, and my brother and I would eat our TV dinners and watch *The Mickey Mouse Club*.

One summer night, Mom invited two neighborhood ladies to watch my brother and me perform two plays, *Hansel and Gretel* and *The Three Little Pigs*. Still, the big treat of the night was that we all got our own TV dinner to eat at the picnic table. What fun!

KATHLEEN McDONALD • WATERFORD, PA

You dropped in a coin and pushed a few buttons, and out came the latest tunes from top bands.

WHAT THE LOCALS ATE AT THE DAIRY BAR

WHEN I WAS YOUNG, MY FOLKS ALWAYS took me to visit my grandparents in Lansing, Ohio. My favorite place to hang out with my friends was Krob's Dairy Bar on Route 40. Everyone went there for the food—hamburgers, ice cream, cherry Cokes, and homemade soups and chili.

Older kids would come in after ballgames to hang out and play songs on the jukebox. Every once in a while, future baseball greats Phil and Joe Niekro would visit the dairy bar.

Other times, we would see future basketball star John Havlicek come in and sit at the counter. The guys were always friendly and polite.

My friends and I sat and giggled while we listened to their conversations. Phil, Joe and John lived in Lansing. At that time, we didn't know how famous they would become. We only wanted to know what these guys ordered to eat. Sometimes they would speak to us, and that made our day.

Sadly, the old dairy bar isn't open anymore, but the owner, Jim Krob, still lives in Lansing.

ROSEMARY GRON · SMITHFIELD, OH

JUKEBOX JAZZ

Some say the word jukebox is from the African word *jook*, meaning "to dance." Others say it derives from "juke joint," referring to a dive or roadside bar.

....

By 1940, there was a jukebox in almost every restaurant and bar in the country.

....

Jukeboxes were popularized in the 1930s and '40s and hit their heyday in the 1950s.

....

In 1941, the war effort required Wurlitzer factories to stop using metal and plastics in its jukeboxes and revert production to war-related goods.

....

Wurlitzer's Paul Fuller designed highly prized jukeboxes, conveying art deco motifs with plastic, glass and wood.

FRIDAY AND SATURDAY AT "THE REC"

My town had a recreation place in the late '50s and early '60s called the Wigwam, but all the kids in town called it "the Rec." Teenagers could go there on Friday and Saturday nights and dance to a jukebox, play pool or Ping-Pong, watch TV, play board games or read comic books.

On Friday nights the kids would dress casually, and on Saturday nights the girls would dress up. The seventh- and eighth-graders could stay only until 9 p.m., while the high school kids could stay until closing at 11 p.m. The place had a huge bar serving pop and snacks, and a huge dance floor with booths all around.

It was supervised, so our parents thought it was a good place for us to socialize with other kids. No kids from out of town could come unless as a guest of a local teenager. Oh, the memories that were made there.

ELOISE ZUBER
WAPAKONETA, OH

THE LOYAL GANG

If you wanted to find your friends on a weekend during the 1950s in Bamberg, South Carolina, Frye's Corner was the first place to begin your search. This picture is of Frye's most loyal gang. From left: Bobby Clary, Tommy Bunch, Jimmy Kemp, Guy Everhart, LittleBoy Jones, Gene Sandifer, Ken Hartley and Sonny Beard.

GUY EVERHART
LEXINGTON, NC

"DON'T BE CRUEL"

As a high school freshman in the mid-'50s, I would occasionally go to a diner called Pat's Grill. I'd hand the waitress a dollar and order a slice of banana cream pie and a glass of milk (90 cents total!). My dime change went directly into the jukebox. When Elvis Presley (right) began singing "Don't Be Cruel," that was my cue to eat. It didn't get any better than that.

RONALD CRAIG
WILLITS, CA

What a classic photo of the gang! Milli is standing with her arms crossed.

Hanging at the Luncheonette

My father, Nick, partnered with his friend Pippi in 1952 and bought a luncheonette on Courtlandt Avenue in the Bronx. They sold sandwiches, fresh baked goods, coffee, and different kinds of soda. There was a candy counter with a glass case and glass shelves. For a penny, a child could choose from a myriad of confections.

What would a luncheonette be without a jukebox spinning the latest 78 rpm records? Every week, the jukebox guy would come to change the songs to popular offerings. I remember "Come On-A My House" by Rosemary Clooney, "Cry" by Johnnie Ray and "You Belong to Me" by Jo Stafford.

My Grandmother Frances and I worked the store when my father and his partner couldn't. I was in my early teens, and it was thrilling to check out the guys who hung around!

They were all so cute with their peg pants and pocket combs. I wasn't allowed to mingle, but when Grandma wasn't around, I flirted.

Weekends in the luncheonette gave me the opportunity to meet girlfriends. Dungarees were just coming into style, and we loved wearing them with flat shoes, sweaters and ponytails.

On summer nights, the whole neighborhood would be outside dealing cards, roller-skating, playing street games, or sitting on stoops and folding chairs. In 1953, the neighborhood started to change, and my father and his partner sold the store. I can still close my eyes and picture the luncheonette and a young teenager wearing tight jeans, flat shoes and a ponytail, dancing to her favorite songs and dreaming about that special guy.

MILLI STELLATOS · MONTVALE, NJ

SHE DRESSED FOR SUCCESS

Standing next to husband Dayo (top left photo), **JOY THOMPSON**, 20, wears her best dress on May 9, 1950, for a ceremony at Illinois State University recognizing scholastic achievement. Joy holds Mark, their first-born child. "I realize now what a special day this was in a young woman's life," writes Joy's daughter **LISA KRALL**, of Dewey, Illinois. "She maintained a high grade point through the stresses of marriage, pregnancy and motherhood. I'd say she did it with grace and style!"

GOOD DESIGN NEVER GOES OUT OF STYLE

WILMA HAWES CONNELY stands next to the suit she bought (near left) for $20 and wore for her marriage in 1952 to Dennis Connely (far left). Purchased at J.C. Penney in Neosho, Missouri, the outfit was displayed at a Penney store in Tulsa, Oklahoma, as part of the company's 100th anniversary. "She will never part with that dress," says daughter **CONNIE CONNELY** of Tulsa.

FAMILY TIE

"Every year at Christmas, I find some occasion to wear it," **BRYCE CLIFTON** of Fremont, Nebraska, says about the silky red tie adorned with artsy, glittery winter scenes. The cheery accessory belonged to Bryce's father, Ray Clifton, in the early 1950s.

A SHARP-DRESSED MAN

Newlyweds (and college students) **ALVIN** and **DORALEE GRIFFITH KLEIN** canoodle in a porch swing at his parents' Wisconsin farm in 1952, top. "I still hug her as much as I did when I wore that pullover!" says Pastor Al, now in his 80s and retired from the ministry in Calhoun, Georgia. He proudly shows off the well-preserved sweater, above.

CHECK NO.	DATE	CHECK ISSUED TO	AMOUNT OF CHECK		√	DATE OF DEP.
949	1/7	T. G. Inc.	50		√	
950	1/9	Dr. Hills - Office Call	5	-	√	
1	1/9	Brotherton's Food Mkt.	1	60	√	
2	1/10	Frankenbergers - Suit - 5 Ties	76	50	√	
3	1/14	T. G. Inc.	50	-	√	

FRUGAL SHOPPER

A. LOVELL ELLIOTT of Barnstable, Massachusetts, strikes a pose in the Harris tweed suit he bought to wear at his new job on Jan. 10, 1950. (He spent $76.50 for the suit and five ties at Frankenberger's—an upscale haberdashery in Charleston, West Virginia.) "My reasons for keeping it are practical," he says. "I'm of Scottish origin."

STILL HER FAVORITE

MARION "DOLLY" TRAHAN of Port Neches, Texas, models the black coat she bought in Louisiana in 1957. "It was my favorite," Dolly says, noting the stylish pushup sleeves, the buttonless closure and a black bow on the back. "When I got married and moved to Texas, the coat came with me."

GROWN-UP GLASSES

I usually had durable glasses that weren't stylish. But when I saw my fifth-grade teacher's cat's-eye frames, I had to have some. I did tire of them, but for a few months in 1958 I just felt so sophisticated.
RANDI DELL · MINERAL WELLS, TX

WEST POINT ATTIRE

Cadet **JIM JENKINS** stands at attention while wearing the dress gray tunic and white trousers required at West Point in 1953. His wife, **BARB JENKINS**, still has the uniform hanging in her closet in Manitowoc, Wisconsin. "He was the cutest guy in our eighth-grade class," she recalls about their early days in nearby Green Bay.

50 YEARS PRESERVED

EARLEEN SUNDAY JOHNSON, 3, above, sports a pink coat and matching hat bought by her grandmother in 1958 at Hein's Department Store in Waukegan, Illinois. Earleen's mother, Betty Sunday, saved the coat for the toddler's future daughters to wear. "Well, I had four wonderful sons," says Earleen, who now lives in Libertyville, Illinois. "The beautiful coat that my mom so carefully preserved for more than 50 years finally was unwrapped and worn by my granddaughters." One of them, Haley, is shown below, clutching her stuffed lamb.

FORK FAKE-OUT

It was typical in the '50s and '60s for boys to wear corduroy pants—or at least that's what my mother kept telling me. By seventh grade, I was embarrassed to wear them, especially because I was growing fast. The pants always seemed to be too short, which prompted the other students to dub them "flood pants."

So I came up with a plan. I bent an old fork and hung it from my breast pocket. That way, I thought, people would look at the fork and not at my too-short, old-fashioned slacks. Problem solved!

It wasn't a great idea, I know, but I was in seventh grade. Actually, it might have worked if, when asked why I was wearing a fork, I hadn't said, "To keep you from noticing my ridiculous corduroy pants."

BRUCE DANIELSON
CAMBRIDGE, MN

BEWARE THE GIRDLE

Playtex rubber girdles were a craze in college in the early '50s. All of us gals had one. Putting the girdle on was a tug-of-war, and wearing it was pure torture. There were holes all over it, but it got hotter and hotter as time went on. Gallantly, we suffered through.

As the girdles aged, they would turn yellow and then brown. Brown meant the item was on its last legs.

One of my friend's girdles exploded during Sunday Mass. Getting outside was a feat in itself, as was suppressing the giggles. On the lawn, our screams of laughter broke the pious morning. Thank God for spandex!

SONIA SCHORK
SIERRA VISTA, AZ

WHITE BUCKS AND DUCKTAILS

AFTER A FEW HIGH SCHOOL classmates of mine began to wear white buck shoes in the 1950s, I knew I had to have a pair. My mom told me they'd be difficult to clean, but she finally gave in. I was so happy!

One major task in getting ready for Sunday Mass was polishing our shoes. Black and brown shoes were no problem, but those white bucks of mine turned out to be a nuisance. As they became more worn, they required more elbow grease to polish. What a chore!

The other laughable trend back then was the ducktail hairdo. Many a young man succumbed to that style. I had a ducktail for a short time.

I still smile at the memories of white bucks, ducktails, sock hops and teenagers loving life.

STAN E. MILLER · LUCK, WI

IN STYLE

Vintage Ads

Whether you were a businessman at the airport or a mother-to-be at the beach, there was no excuse not to be stylish.

The suit that *looks* right and *feels* right when you first try it on is most likely the one that will be best for you. A suit that fits will conform to your figure without any strain anywhere, whether you're sitting, standing or stretching. How can you find such a suit? Go to the dealer who sells Hart Schaffner & Marx clothes. He not only wants to find the right suit for you...he is best able to do so. He is able to select from the 253 different combinations of sizes and shapes that we make.

This is the famous Pan American suit in the three-button, patch pocket model. There are, of course, other models, patterns and colors.

HART SCHAFFNER & MARX

HERE'S A RARE signed ad from commercial illustrator Tom Hall, who handled the print advertising account for Chicago suit-maker Hart Schaffner & Marx for almost 20 years. His men's apparel ads often featured, as this one, an urbane man going about his work while a pretty woman (or two) admired him from afar. The small print indicates the man wears the "Pan American," a suit style Hart Schaffner & Marx designed using South American wools.

Maternity ensemble by Simonetta. One of a series created for Mennen by noted designers.

To Every Lady-in-Waiting

You can protect baby's skin as nature does at birth with our exclusive-formula Baby Magic

STOPS DIAPER RASH...CHAFING...CHAPPING Cover your baby's skin from head to toe with Mennen Baby Magic to help protect against infection. It actually forms an invisible "bodyguard" that effectively destroys the bacteria that cause diaper rash. Nature protects this way at birth!

Many leading hospitals use Baby Magic the moment nature's protection is washed off! The next time you see your doctor, ask him about protective pink Baby Magic...used by more mothers than any other baby lotion.

PREVENTS DIAPER RASH when used regularly. Baby Magic heals it, too. Prevents prickly heat. Giant size, $1. Squeeze bottle, 60¢.

ANTICHAFING POWDER! Resists perspiration and diaper moisture. Clings longer, too. Refreshes baby from head to toe. 35¢ and 59¢.

baby oil

baby powder

BABY CLEANSING OIL! For oil baths until navel heals. Use regularly to cleanse diaper area without harsh rubbing. 55¢ and $1.

ALL TAX FREE

for babies its Mennen

MENNEN TAKES a different tack from competitor Johnson & Johnson in this *Life* ad. Instead of a fussy baby, it shows a mother-to-be in a chic maternity outfit by designer Simonetta. Becoming a mom doesn't mean giving up style.

THE EPITOME OF COOL: LEATHER JACKETS

By the mid-1950s, leather jackets had reached such infamy that certain styles were banned from schools. Still, the jackets soared in popularity, and some retailers guessed the bans helped increase sales. But even if you could sneak your leather past the principal, our readers say the hardest part was getting clearance from Mom and Dad.

AN EARLY LEATHER LOVE

My first leather was a classic motorcycle jacket—rough and rugged with all the zippers and pockets. My brother let me pick it out at the Harley-Davidson store. I think it cost about $100. The leather squeaked and cracked as I moved around, but I was the envy of my peers. No one else had that type of jacket. I wore it for three years before it became too small for me. As I've gotten older, I've bought three similar jackets, but none of them had the ruggedness and feel of the first. I still think about it from time to time. Thanks, brother!

EUGENE STALLABY · OKLAHOMA CITY, OK

WORTH THE WAIT

I wanted a leather jacket in elementary school after seeing Marlon Brando in the movie *The Wild One*. My parents gave me a firm no.

As I got into my teens, I still wanted one, but Mom and Dad again thought I'd look like a juvenile delinquent. A leather jacket in those days gave that impression. I just wanted to look cool!

By the time I got married, in the '70s, I had pretty much forgotten about leather jackets. There was still a part of me that wanted one, but it was no big deal.

Finally, in the '80s, I got a leather jacket for Christmas—from my parents, no less! I think the Fonz and *Happy Days* might have warmed them up to the idea. After all, Fonzie turned out to be a nice guy. The jacket was one of the best gifts I ever got and gave me a thrill for all the years I owned it.

DANNY ATCHLEY · MINERAL WELLS, TX

ALL THANKS TO MOM

I got my leather jacket when I was in ninth grade, in 1955. The school—Franklin Junior High School in Green Bay, Wisconsin—said black leather jackets would not be allowed. Because of all the biker movies out at the time, I thought the rule meant the ones with zippers and studs. My jacket was plain—it predated the Fonz's but was the same one that he later wore.

My mother bought the jacket for me, and I quickly wrote my name on the liner so it couldn't be returned. When I debuted my leather look at school, the principal called my mother and told her it was not in line with the dress code! She told him it was a nice jacket and I was going to wear it. Common sense prevailed, and plain leather jackets were allowed.

FRED GIESLER SR. · TWO RIVERS, WI

GOING OUT IN STYLE

This group of pals from Selden Rural High School in Selden, Kansas, poses for a photo wearing matching leather jackets (and dangling cigarettes) in 1957. The photo was snapped at a going-away party.

DIANA FOWLER · WICHITA, KS

MARLON BRANDO

BATHING BEAUTIES

Swimwear fads are ever-changing, and the 1950s styles definitely started to shake things up. For many then, and now, a swimsuit had less to do with actual swimming and more to do with looking good on a beach or at a local pool, like a pinup. But no matter what was worn, as you can tell by the photos here, folks were having fun!

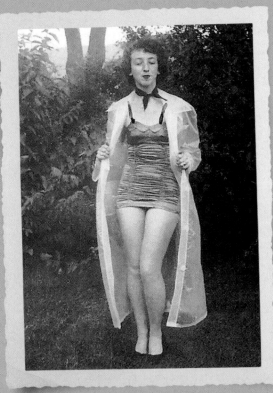

IT'S THE RAINCOAT THAT MAKES IT

It was a cold fall day in Vermont in 1950 when I honored my boyfriend's request for a pinup photo. He was stationed at Keesler Air Force Base in Biloxi, Mississippi, and it was the first time we had been separated since we'd become neighbors at age 10. In an effort to ward off frostbite, I added a clear plastic raincoat over the bathing suit. The suit was strapless, so I enhanced the finished photo with inked-in straps. Why? Who knows? But he never complained. It must have worked, since we've been married for more than 60 years.
CLAIRE LACROIX ESPOSITO · MIDDLETOWN, OH

PYRAMID SCHEMES

My first husband, Bill Muster, was a fine photographer, and he seemed to enjoy taking pictures of me. In the early 1950s, we lived in Hollywood and frequently drove south to Laguna Beach on Sundays with a group of friends to enjoy the California sun and fun. Building human pyramids was something that happened more often than not. That's me on the bottom of the pyramid on the far left.
PAULA HASSLER · TEMPE, AZ

STILL SURFING
This photo of me (top) was taken in 1956, while I was surfing at Waikiki, Hawaii. Fifty-four years later, I returned to the island and re-created my first visit. (If you think I've changed, check out the landscape behind me!)
ROBERT MEEHAN
BIG BEAR LAKE, CA

OOH-LA-LA!
Dad was an international civil engineer, and we lived all over the world. Because he traveled heavily, I spent much of my formative years in boarding school. Here I am in the south of France in the late '50s. This photo illustrates why a father would keep his teenage daughter locked away in boarding school!
MARIANNA WILKINSON · VIA EMAIL

CRAZY FOR CAPRIS

Capri pants (aka pedal pushers) emerged in the 1950s as a casual clothing alternative. Invented in 1948 by European designer Sonja de Lennart and named for one of her favorite island destinations, the slacks were made popular by female celebrities and quickly became a household staple for American women. Grace Kelly and Audrey Hepburn pioneered the trend in film; on TV, Mary Tyler Moore led a crusade on *The Dick Van Dyke Show*, sporting the pants that she herself wore regularly. Today, capris still endure in women's (and even men's) wardrobes.

SHE HAD THE LOOK
Here I am wearing my favorite capri pants in May 1958 in Lakeland, Florida. The shoes (flats) were typical of that era too. I would not be caught dead wearing either style now, but they were certainly fun to wear then!
BETTY VICKERS · ST. GEORGE, UT

VACATION PANTS
During the mid-1950s, my cousin Bonnie Sue's parents asked me to accompany them on their summer vacation to a cottage they rented on a lake in Michigan. Our attire was usually pedal pushers—no wet pant legs from wading and no sunburned thighs from sitting in a rowboat!
JEANNE FLANDERS
NOBLESVILLE, IN

PRETTY IN PINK

I have enjoyed lots of fishing trips and picnics with my family. I was 17 years old here, wearing my capris next to a trout stream and our 1958 Pontiac.
JUDY THOMPSON · ANKENY, IA

GOING PLAID

In this photo, my baby sister, Valerie, and I were visiting our great-grandmother in Vero Beach, Florida, in 1958. I was 18, and she was 3.
JANET KLIVEN
ROMOLAND, CA

BRIGHT STATEMENT

Magenta was the color to have in 1957. In this photo, I'm washing my '57 Chevy in my new magenta capris while my sister, Betty, inspects my work. I wish I had a 1957 Chevy golf cart today—then I could come full circle with that wonderful car! I would drive it around our community wearing the capris of today.
SANDY HOLIHAN FRITZ · AURORA, CO

Colonel Sanders Found His Calling: Chicken

When we fell in love with fast food in the 1950s, someone already had a leg up and was waiting in the wings.

Harland Sanders, born in 1890, was a streetcar conductor, justice of the peace, steamboat ferry operator and insurance salesman before he started serving folks fried chicken from his own table while operating a service station in Corbin, Kentucky, in 1930.

Curious by nature, he experimented with herbs and spices for his chicken and also tried cooking it under pressure to serve folks faster.

His fame grew, and in 1935, he was made an honorary Kentucky colonel in recognition of his contributions to the state's cuisine. When a new highway bypassed his restaurant in the early 1950s, he sold his operation and lived briefly on Social Security checks.

Confident of his product, the Colonel began franchising his chicken business in 1952, entering into handshake agreements with restaurant owners who paid him a nickel for each chicken they sold.

When he sold the operation in 1964, there were more than 600 franchised outlets. By 1971, there were more than 3,500 KFC restaurants around the world. He remained a public spokesman for KFC until his death in 1980, traveling 250,000 miles a year visiting the empire he founded.

Colonel Sanders stood by his product and the international fast food empire that is KFC until his death.

Holy Hoops!

Benedictine sisters at the convent of Christ the King Catholic School in Oklahoma City, Oklahoma, got into the swing of things in 1958 as the Hula-Hoop craze swept through the country.

AFTER SETTLING a friendly sibling squabble at an airport in the 1950s, American Airlines flight attendant Jean Hoder found herself at the center of the kids' attention. Jean's story is on page 112.

AT WORK

The workforce was changing and
new amenities and luxuries like
air travel provided more jobs.

Location, Location, Location

Working as a secretary, I was 23 when I got a job in 1954 with the leasing agent of a large company in downtown Chicago, Illinois. We worked with many stores and other businesses to offer them space in a new venture—an open shopping mall called Hillside Center in the western suburb of Hillside, Illinois. Little did I know that this would be the first large major shopping mall in the Chicago suburbs.

The work was fascinating and I loved it. We entered into leases with Carson Pirie Scott & Co., Goldblatt's department store, and various small businesses that were anxious to try out the new and very different site.

The mall opened in September 1956, and by then, we had acquired leases from more than 60 businesses. This concept was so unique to the area that thousands of people turned out on opening day to experience the new way of shopping.

Other suburban malls followed, including Oakbrook Center in Oak Brook and Yorktown Center in Lombard, but, unfortunately, these stores pulled customers away from Hillside Center.

When I went back for a visit years later, the majority of stores had moved out. A Menards had replaced what was once Goldblatt's, and a DMV office and a magazine newsstand that had been there from the very beginning were the only businesses left inside the mall.

Today, that Menards has closed and most of the mall has been demolished.

MARILYN CELESCHI · MADISON, WI

The Shops of Grand Avenue in downtown Milwaukee, Wisconsin, occupy a site once graced by a hotel and an arcade. The plaza welcomed visitors to shop, eat or watch a fashion show, as seen here in August 1983. Today, the Shops await a rebirth to include office space and a ground-level food hall featuring local food and beverage vendors.

STRETCHING THE TRUTH

IF YOU AREN'T FAMILIAR WITH STEAK STRETCHERS, you probably never worked in a small-town grocery store in the 1950s. I grew up in Stephenville, Texas, and there were four neighborhood grocers around the courthouse square. My first job was at Minter's, as a clerk.

On my first day, the Minter's butchers, Elmer and Doyle, stalled me at the door. "Before you put your apron on, Jack, run across the street to Moser's and get our steak stretcher back. I loaned it to him last week."

I followed orders, and the Moser's butcher told me he had loaned the stretcher to Williams' grocery around the corner. From there, it was routed to Stigler's. Two sweaty hours later, the Stigler's butcher said he'd sent the steak stretcher back to Minter's. Everyone laughed as the rookie returned, sans stretcher. With a red face, I realized two things: I had passed my initiation, and there was no such thing as a steak stretcher.

Two weeks later, Minter's hired a new clerk, and sure enough, Elmer's first words to him: "Marvin, before you put your apron on…" You know the rest of the story.

JACK HICKEY • SPRING, TX

GOING UP!

In Flint, Michigan, in 1951, I gave up an office job making $25 a week to run the elevator at JCPenney for $37.50 a week. The store gave us two tan blouses and skirts for fall, and white skirts with white-and-green striped blouses for summer. We stood outside the door and said, "Going up," until we had enough people. The passengers called out their floors, and as we arrived, I'd announce, "Second floor, ladies and girls." Then I opened the gate and pulled on a lever to open the door. There was no automation—it was all muscle power.

I liked interacting with people, especially at Christmas, when everyone was in a good mood and didn't mind if you crowded people in. I remember one man had to hold a sled over his head!

MARILYN HENDERSON
ALPENA, MI

SNAKE IN THE GRASS

In the summer of 1951, I was 23 years old, working part time as a lifeguard at a small lake in Sand Springs, Oklahoma. The beach was open until 10 p.m. or until everyone left. This particular Sunday was extremely hot and unusually busy. About 9 p.m., I told my co-worker Stan that I was going to take a walk. No one was in the water, but there were a lot of couples lying around on towels necking.

I found a thicket of reeds where the ground seemed to be moving. A harmless grass snake had just given birth to dozens of little snake babies, each one about the size of a pencil. I started picking them up between my fingers until I had about a dozen.

As I walked back up the beach, I slowly dropped a snake here and there. "Get ready to go home," I told Stan back at the tower. He looked confused—until we heard the scream: "Snake!"

Within five minutes, the beach was empty. We went home early.

BILL SKELTON • PARK RAPIDS, MN

One Hectic Night in the ER

Mistakes aside, her transfer of duty came as a welcome relief.

After I graduated in 1954 from Naval Hospital Corps School in Great Lakes, Illinois, I was assigned to the Navy hospital at Camp Pendleton, California. My first assignment was night duty in the emergency room. We were busy that first night. The pregnant wife of a Marine came in ready to deliver. The doctor told me to prepare her for an examination.

Well, being a very green recruit fresh out of school with no experience, I had the woman take off all her clothes. That was my first mistake.

The doctor's face got red with anger and he shouted, "I just wanted to see how far apart her contractions were!"

In a sarcastic voice he then asked if I thought I could locate a stretcher. Again, being green, I started looking for a stretcher. When I had a hard time finding one, I should have known something was wrong. I looked up and down the long hallways before finally finding a stretcher hanging on a wall. After cleaning off all the spiderwebs, I headed back to the ER. That was my second mistake.

The impatient doctor took one look at the stretcher and yelled,

"Any idiot would know I meant a gurney!"

At school we'd been taught the difference between a stretcher and a gurney. He went on to say at the top of his voice, "I ought to make you carry this naked woman all by yourself to the delivery room!"

As you might guess, it didn't take long before I was transferred out of the ER. I wound up in charge of the medical unit, working the night shift alone with six or seven patients.

But I was in California, with its beautiful beaches and a handsome young sailor to distract me. Who had time to sleep while off duty?

One night it got especially quiet at work; all the patients were sleeping. Struggling to stay awake, I spread a magazine across the edge of a narrow medical sink.

The next thing I knew, I felt water splashing my face. I had fallen asleep with my head in the sink and someone had turned on the water.

I checked all the patients, who were still fast asleep. I checked the hallways but no one was there. I never found out who turned on the water, but believe me, I was wide awake the rest of the shift.

LOUISE PIERCE
TUPELO, MS

Louise, shown sprawling on a stack of books, found a certain sailor quite distracting in California. They wed some 60 years ago; he's still distracting.

Young fellas, top, gathered at the Cozy Corner cafe, run by David's parents, to listen to St. Bonaventure basketball games on the radio. Regulars sat on the front porch, left, to chat about local events and politics.

COZYING UP TO THE BAR

MY TEEN YEARS BACK IN THE EARLY '50s WERE spent sweeping floors and cleaning tables while my parents, Art and Mary Ann, operated a soda shop called the Cozy Corner. Located in our small town of Olean, New York, the Cozy Corner was widely known.

It really was a cozy place, just as Mom and Dad hoped it would be. Hot dogs were 15 cents, soda floats were 20 cents, and eggs, toast and coffee were a bargain at 35 cents. People stopped by the shop to relax, read the newspapers, and share conversation over a treat while listening to music from the sensational colorfully lit 20-record jukebox. To me, these Cozy Corner photos (above) depict a peaceful time of life in America.

DAVID FORNEY • OLEAN, NY

THE JERK AND THE REDHEAD

It was the summer of 1950, and I had just graduated from high school. Grandpa Ruben Dickinson played cards with Frank Kellner, who had recently installed a soda fountain at his drugstore and needed help.

Thanks to my grandpa, Mr. Kellner hired me as his soda jerk. I learned quickly how to make all the sundaes and sodas, but it took a lot of practice to get the malted milk container off the mixer without spraying myself and everything nearby. I got to be an expert at cleaning up.

I met a lot of nice people—two young guys in particular. One was short with dark, curly hair and another was tall with red hair. When the weather got cold the redhead's nose would turn red, and he wore an ugly green overcoat that he had inherited from a cousin.

I guess I didn't mind the coat too much, because by Christmas I was dating the redhead, whose name was Curtis. And, yes, I married him.

LOIS SUNSTROM-LOVERING
STURGEON BAY, WI

An unusual assortment of sounds went into the re-creation of Priscilla's blast.

A Gun, a Wall and a Waterfall

With 20 minutes to airtime, a sound-effects artist had to reproduce a noise he'd never heard—the detonation of an atomic bomb.

I had created thunder and rain, Times Square on New Year's Eve—I'd fooled millions of people as a sound-effects artist. But one night in 1957, I had to come up with a sound that would fool even myself.

I'd been doing the sound effects for a popular soap opera at the time when on June 24, 1957, I had to fill in on NBC's 6 p.m. newscast. Most news films didn't require much sound sweetening, but the need was serious on this historic night. Viewers would see the detonation of an atomic bomb.

In the newsroom, I watched the blaze mushrooming in clouds of dust, reaching upward ominously.

"What happened to the sound?" I asked the film editor.

He said the blast had melted all of the sound engineer's microphones. Then the editor looked at the clock and said I had 20 minutes to re-create the sound of that bomb.

In the sound-effects library, I grabbed three recordings: a naval gun firing over water, an iron ball smashing a brick wall, and an African waterfall. I slowed them down on the turntable until I was satisfied they matched what I imagined the sound to be and, just as important, the fireball's menacing pace.

As nervous as I'd been, after my sound creation aired, the NBC executives didn't complain—even the scientists who created the atomic bomb didn't complain! Who knows? Maybe the effects I played that night really did sound like the bomb. After all, I've fooled millions of people. Were you one of them?

ROBERT L. MOTT · ARROYO GRANDE, CA

THE NEVADA TEST SITE

The footage Robert "sweetened with sound" was the broadcast of the Priscilla shot, part of Operation Plumbbob, at the Nevada Test Site north of Las Vegas.

....

The flash from the site's first detonation, on Jan. 27, 1951, could be seen as far away as San Francisco.

....

In 1955, Survival Town—a group of houses and other structures filled with mannequins—was built near ground zero to learn how buildings would withstand a blast.

....

Over more than 40 years, the U.S. conducted 928 atmospheric and underground nuclear tests at the site.

....

The last test detonated underground on Sept. 23, 1992.

....

Should U.S. nuclear testing resume, the now-renamed Nevada National Security Site is ready for action.

WORKING ROUND THE CLOCK

IN THE SUMMER OF 1951, I WAS 11, but because I was tall for my age— 5 feet 10 inches—our paper carrier offered me a job delivering the *Kansas City Star* and *Times*. The pay was $11.50 a week, which sure beat my 25-cent allowance.

The job involved tossing rolled-up papers to houses from the back of a 1948 half-ton Chevy pickup truck, and delivering the papers by hand to apartments. I would share duties with an older boy while the boss drove. I'd have to arrive by 3:30 a.m. for morning delivery and 3 p.m. for afternoon.

After much debate, my mom said I could try it for a couple of weeks. I soon found out I was responsible for delivering nearly 600 newspapers to 315 street residences and almost 300 apartment dwellers living in 10-story apartment buildings on the Country Club Plaza in Kansas City, Missouri.

I learned to wrap papers on the go, throw them more than 150 feet while the truck was moving, and exit the moving truck to pick up a paper that had come apart. I could tie-wrap up to 32 papers a minute using a crank machine and deliver 88 papers to the apartments in less than nine minutes.

All in all, I felt a sense of grown-up pride that I was fulfilling a job, rubbing elbows with deliverymen and meeting people from all walks of life. I walked to work in the early mornings and, for a time, it seemed the city was asleep and I was the only one awake.

I quit the route in 1953. But those early lessons stayed with me my whole life.

BARRY R. DAVIS · GRAVOIS MILLS, MO

WORD TO THE WISE GUY

FROM 1953 UNTIL THE DAY I LEFT for college in 1959, I had a Sunday paper route. I delivered the papers in the early morning and then went back to collect money around 10 a.m.

My last stop was Cowboy's Saloon, which had a pinball machine. In those days, all taverns in Pennsylvania had to be closed on Sundays. Every booze joint in the coal region ignored the law; you just had to enter through a side or back door. Thus, having a 16-year-old paperboy take the side entrance for payment on a Sunday was no big deal.

Cowboy's machine had a grid of five rows of five random numbers. To win, you had to get three or more of the same number in a row. One Sunday, I hit five in a row— a first in my pinball career.

"I won, Cowboy," I told him. "Give me five bucks."

"No!" Cowboy retorted. "Yer not supposed to be gambling."

I could be a wise guy, so I shot back, "I'm not supposed to be in your saloon, either."

Still grumbling, Cowboy forked over the cash.

The next day, I took the five clams to a bookstore and bought a brand-new hardbound thumb-indexed dictionary. I used it throughout high school, college and my career as an author and comic strip artist.

PATRICK REYNOLDS
WILLOW STREET, PA

Friendly Chats Between Flights

Long layovers flew by fast after three boys became avid fans.

Back in the 1950s, I was a flight attendant with American Airlines. In those days we were called stewardesses. I was based in Chicago and worked either five-city flights to New York City and back, or overnights to the West Coast. The round trips to New York meant that we flew the same trip for several days each week.

Between arrival and return flights, we got to spend a few hours in the lounge or with passengers in the airport. I loved watching the passengers come and go. Some had great smiles on their faces as they greeted a loved one. Others were in tears as they bid someone goodbye. The downtime between flights gave us flight attendants a chance to meet people who wanted to talk or who seemed a bit nervous because this was their first flight.

One day at LaGuardia Airport in New York, I noticed three young boys having a scuffle of some sort. I spoke to them about settling down or they might be asked to leave the area. Much to my surprise, they started asking questions about who I was, why I was there, and where I was going. These boys were not the least bit shy. As we talked, I offered to buy each of them a soda and some candy.

By this time, they were somewhat entranced and we began a pleasant conversation. My layover was three hours and the time flew by. The boys waited for me to board my flight and waved goodbye when we took off.

The very next day, like clockwork, the boys were there to greet me when my flight landed. This time they looked particularly neat with their hair nicely combed and big smiles on their precious young faces. We had apparently bonded and were now good friends. Our relationship continued for as long as I was on the same schedule, and I looked forward to our reunions as much as they did. Sometimes they'd bring a sister or a cousin to join us.

Jean was 28 when Gallagher brothers Dennis, 10, and Brian, 9, buddy Artie Hicks, 8, and another friend started an airport fan club.

I looked forward to our reunions as much as they did.

A bystander who observed what was going on must have called the newspaper, because the next thing I remember, we were having our photos taken and the children were being given a complete tour of the aircraft.

Recently I celebrated my 87th birthday. As I reflected over the years and all the memories of a lifetime, this story stood out. It was one of my favorite times. So often I have wondered how and where those boys are now. I wonder if they remember, as I do, this very special friendship we had so many years ago.

JEAN HODER · HANSON, MA

ON THE JOB

Vintage Ads

Women were stepping into the workforce more and more in the 1950s, bringing home extra money for their families.

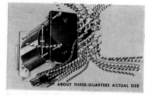

Sally doesn't solder any more...

and that benefits Bell telephone users

AN AD from the 1950s shows "Sally" at work demonstrating an innovative new development from Bell Telephone Laboratories and Western Electric. The "gun" (shown) wraps wires on telephone equipment so tightly that solder isn't needed. That the ad shows a woman at work testifies to the growing number of women in the workforce.

WOMEN MADE money at home in the 1950s by having Tupperware parties and by selling Doehla All-Occasion Greeting Card and Stationery Assortments to friends, neighbors and co-workers. It was something that could be done full time or in one's spare time, which worked for many homemakers.

1950

STEP INTO THE PAST

It's 1950, and the Hastings are ready to serve you at their Arrowsmith, Illinois, grocery. "We sold everything," writes former employee **DOROTHY WAGNER**. "Clothes, nails, meats, you name it."

NICE PENMANSHIP

This photo was taken at General Mitchell International Airport, in Milwaukee, Wisconsin, in 1959. I am on the left. This is how we made reservations for American Airlines flights—every passenger received a handwritten ticket. Notice there's not a computer in sight!
PATRICIA LYNCH MARKS
GERMANTOWN, WI

BEHIND THE SCENES AT DAIRY QUEEN

AFTER I GRADUATED FROM HIGH SCHOOL IN 1950, I was looking for a job, and my dad told me about a new business opening across the street from where he worked that needed help. I applied and was hired to work at one of the first Dairy Queens in Ohio.

Because they wanted to open the store as soon as possible, I got a crash course on what to do and how to make the soft serve, as it was called. The process started in a machine that had to be immaculately clean. The store had two of these machines, and it was my job to clean and set them up.

Each had an auger that was about 4 feet long and very heavy, which I oiled with a petroleum paste. Then I assembled the machines and poured in the prepared mix that made up the Dairy Queen soft serve.

It took about four hours—cleaning plus freezing time—before a machine was ready for serving. Meanwhile, I made sure the store was spotless, well-supplied and ready for business. I started at 7 a.m., and the store opened at noon.

A young woman worked the window. She would serve from one machine until it got close to empty, then switch to the other machine while I cleaned the first one again.

The person who owned the business was from Cadiz, Ohio, and he was said to be in partnership with none other than Clark Gable, the actor. They had gone to school together in Cadiz.

The business went so well that in a short time a second store opened. I'd be at one store in the morning and the second one in the afternoon. Soon, I trained other men to keep the machines running so I didn't have to run back and forth as much. I made a whopping 75 cents an hour. I thought I was rich when it went up to a dollar!

FRED L. WISE
NEWARK, OH

CLASS DISTINCTION
I graduated from high school in 1951, and I met my husband in 1959, so my favorite decade has to be—you guessed it—the 1950s.

I went to college at Syracuse University, where it was all business and traditions. Women dressed in heels, skirts, gloves and, often, hats, and we all worked hard.

Imagine my shock when I began teaching in 1956 and bumped head-on into the rock 'n' roll generation. Two college degrees had not prepared me for ducktails, greased hair, suede shoes and boys' pink-striped pants in my eighth-grade classroom. But I reached them. The kids wished me well when I moved to Florida in 1959 to take another teaching position.

That fall, I met Don Schork, a Korean War vet who taught American history. We dated all year; chaperoned games, dances and club events; and married at the end of the school year. The class of 1960 claimed responsibility for our getting married. I guess they did a good job, because we're still together more than 50 years later.
SONIA SCHORK · SIERRA VISTA, AZ

When the Shoe
Shop Shined

I'd like to share this 1950 photo of my grandfather Michael Paoello Sr. at work in his shoemaker shop in New York City. He is the first one on the left. Customers would either leave their shoes and leather handbags or simply take a seat and wait for the repaired items.

ELENA PARAVATI · PALISADES PARK, NJ

SOLDIERS POSE in 1951 with an M46 Patton tank, painted to look like a fierce tiger, during the Korean War. The tank held a crew of five: commander, gunner, loader, driver and hull machine gunner.

OUR HEROES

Taking a look back on those who stood up for our nation through the tough times of the decade.

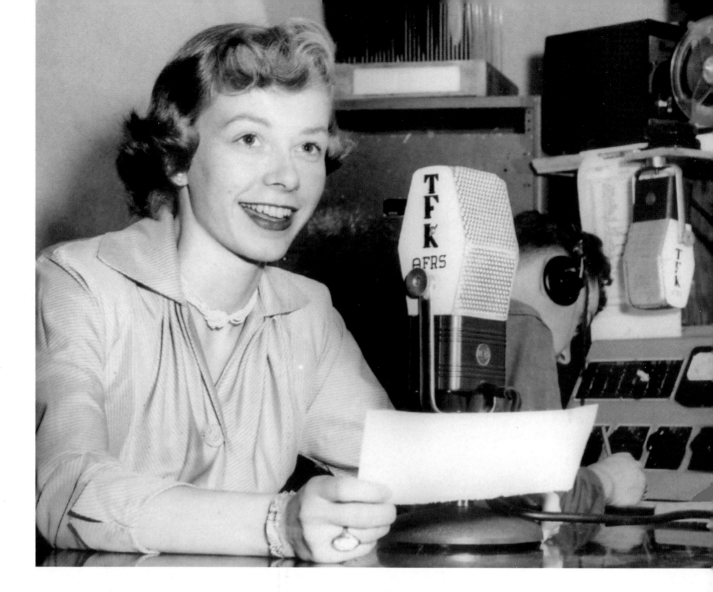

Their Favorite Melody

Servicemen in Iceland couldn't get enough of this charming radio host's show.

Every girl, at some time in her life, should have a chance to feel like the belle of the ball. The months I spent at the U.S. Navy's Keflavik air base in Iceland were mine. The Navy and Air Force personnel on the base knew me as Miss Melody, the voice of a record request show that aired from 10 p.m. to midnight on the Armed Forces Radio Service station TFK in 1952.

There weren't any servicewomen stationed there, and no accommodations for dependents, so I was one of the few American women around. I had followed my husband, Clint, to Iceland after he was accepted to an overseas teaching program.

The men must have been lonely for the sound of an American girl's voice, because my radio show took off. We were so flooded with requests that we had to close the phone lines a couple of hours before airtime each night, and ended up adding an hour to the show.

For such a little station, a great deal of our programming involved live talent, and some of the guys there were exceptional. Len Schiffren had a wonderful voice and personality. The station got large shipments of transcriptions—big records, about the size of a giant pizza—containing radio shows from home that featured favorites like Bob and Ray, Jack Benny and others.

Smitten with Barbara's girl-next-door appeal, servicemen showered her with affection. As Miss Melody (left), she played their favorite songs from TFK and was honored as Miss Plunger (above). Off air, she became friends with fellow radio DJ Len (above, right) and Col. "Red" Elkins (right).

The men were so good to me and treated me like their valued little sister. I was overwhelmed by all of the mail from servicemen, their sweethearts and families back home, and Icelandic citizens. And I was named Miss Tank Platoon and even Miss Plunger.

When I received a letter from the base plumbers telling me that I had been honored as Miss Plunger, I truly thought it was a joke—or perhaps a put-down—and made some humorous reference to it on air. I very quickly got an indignant response telling me that Lana Turner had been proud to be named Miss Plunger and wore a little gold plunger on her charm bracelet to celebrate her exalted status.

After eating a lot of crow on air, I was rewarded the next night with a cake—beautifully decorated, dedicated to "Miss Plunger for Keflavik."

With the approach of fall came news that Clint would be assigned to a new

post in Prestwick, Scotland. The servicemen threw us a big party with dinner, dancing and lots of sentimental speeches. The only letdown was being told that I could not take my fan mail with me because it was technically government property.

Months later, a large package arrived for me at our new apartment with all of those treasured letters. My friend "Boston Bob" Kent—an Air Force baker who kept the radio crew supplied with doughnuts and other goodies—was like a big brother to me, and he had liberated the letters from the filing cabinet at TFK, earning my everlasting gratitude. I still have every one.

BARBARA STOUGHTON
MIDLAND, MI

A Sunny Disposition Captivated the Troops

Orphaned by war, one little girl found an adoptive group of soldiers who treated her like one of their own.

During my stint in Korea, one of my most emotional experiences was the time we spent with a 6-year-old girl we called Sunny. My unit, Company B, was working to improve supply routes, and Sgt. James McIlwain, known to most of us as Hoss, and his engineers were laboring over a road when they heard moans from behind a hedgerow. There the sergeant discovered a little Korean girl who was ill and malnourished and holding her little brother, who was probably half her age.

Through a translator, we learned her story. When the Chinese attacked her home, her mother took her and her brother south, traveling with other displaced Koreans. Just north of Chechon, her mother died, and the two children were separated from the other refugees.

Alone and lost, the girl decided to return home, not realizing it had been destroyed. Carrying her brother, she turned north and followed a river. She found only bits of food. After about a week, she stopped to rest under a tree. Her little brother was extremely weak. This was when our company found the two.

We rushed them to our battalion doctor, Lt. Joseph Blackshear, who put the girl on a liquid diet. Sgt. Pat Aday, a medic, stayed by her side all day and night, feeding her juices.

Tragically, her little brother died a few days later. The girl started to get better, though, and it wasn't long before she was well enough to walk. We started calling her Sunny. As she recovered, she seemed ready to start a new life as the memories of her previous life faded.

The whole company quickly embraced Sunny. Dresses arrived for her from the States. She had

Soldiers found this lost little girl and nursed her back to health.

a front-row seat on movie night, and she always showed up when we played records. Most of us spoke enough Korean to talk with her. She was a wonderful bright spot in our lives, and we loved her like a daughter.

We soon learned that an orphanage in Pusan had room for Sunny, who wasn't told of the arrangements. Only our commanding officer knew when she would leave. When the day came, he had her belongings carefully collected and packed. One of our fellow soldiers, Rupert McElyea, was given the duty of taking Sunny to the orphanage. He loaded her clothes on a truck, then went to find her. "Come on, Sunny," he told her. "Let's go riding."

Normally, Sunny absolutely loved going for rides, but when she saw her things in the truck she jumped out of her seat.

Here was a little girl who had been through a lot and lost everything. She thought she'd found a new family she would have forever. Tears ran down her face. I don't think she understood that we, as soldiers, would have to go home someday.

Our translator struggled to convince her that she would have a better life in a home with other children her own age. Finally, they drove away.

When we returned from work that day, we learned that Sunny had gone to the orphanage. I believe that was the saddest day we spent in Korea. We were quiet, and no one ate much supper. We had lost our ray of sunshine and hadn't even said goodbye.

I went to bed early that night with tears in my eyes. All I could think about was Sunny, the amazing little girl who touched so many hearts.

DALE CASTEEL · ATHENS, AL

Dale holds Sunny, the sweet orphan girl, who wraps her arm around Dale's brother, Jimmy.

She was a wonderful bright spot in our lives, and we loved her like a daughter.

Brothers Dale and Jimmy were in the National Guard in high school before their unit was mobilized into service in 1951.

TIMELINE

SEPTEMBER 1945
After Japan's surrender in WWII liberates Korea, the country is divided at the 38th parallel into North and South.

....

JUNE 25, 1950
The North Korean People's Army, helped by the Soviet Union, invades South Korea.

....

The United Nations Security Council calls for the withdrawal of the NKPA.

....

JUNE 26, 1950
President Harry S. Truman commits U.S. military forces.

....

SEPT. 15, 1950
The U.S.-led U.N. forces start to push the invading North Korean forces northward.

....

OCT. 25, 1950
The Chinese People's Volunteer Army joins the fight, inflicting losses on U.N. forces and driving them out of North Korea. A stalemate follows.

....

JULY 1951
Peace talks begin in Panmunjom.

....

JULY 1953
The Korean War ends with an armistice establishing a demilitarized zone at the 38th parallel. No peace treaty is signed.

....

Nearly 1.8 million Americans fought in the conflict.

GENERAL ASSEMBLY

Jack and I drove to Washington, D.C., for our honeymoon in April 1951. We happened to arrive the day Gen. Douglas MacArthur was returning home from Asia after being fired by President Truman. The place was crowded and we had nowhere to stay. You can see the throng of people behind me in this picture, which was taken with a Gnome Pixie camera.

DOROTHY HUTSON
EAST PROVIDENCE, RI

CAUGHT IN THE ACT

My Kodak No. 2 Folding Cartridge Premo, which I got as a gift in the 1940s, came with me when I entered the Navy in 1950. I snapped pictures at boot camp, on board ship and at stops around the world. I took this shot at Marineland in Florida in 1953.

TOM WILLIAMS • MANHEIM, PA

PINT-SIZE GI

"I'm the shorty," **BOB RIEGEL** admits regarding this 1954 photo taken in Aschaffenburg, Germany. He sure wishes he had kept in touch with his tall buddy, Red Carroll.

PLATOON BUDDIES

GEORGE ESPRAVNIK, right, from Lowell, Indiana, met Ilario Fabbrini in 1951 in Honolulu, Hawaii, while training for the war in Korea. They ended up in the same company and platoon. Their families still keep in touch.

Lt. Jack Hickey kept his helmet close while serving near the 38th parallel in Korea.

Eddie Fisher

An Hourlong Boost for the Troops

Any reminder of home meant a lot to these guys.

During the summer of 1952 I was stationed near Seoul, South Korea, with the 176th Armored Field Artillery Battalion. We received a call that a Special Services division would be arriving shortly after lunch to present an hour of entertainment. They must have gotten wind of our lunch menu and scheduled their arrival after eating with another unit. The farther back you were, the better the chow.

All three batteries and headquarters personnel who could be spared headed to a hillside nearby. A makeshift stage rigged from ammo crates was set up along with audio equipment. A couple of hundred men converged, waiting for the show.

He arrived on schedule—Eddie Fisher, the singing heartthrob who thrilled American teenagers and their moms back home before he answered Uncle Sam's call. The fact that he was assigned to a Special Services unit, considered a soft assignment, mattered little. Here he was, in uniform, in the Army and in Korea. He was one of us and we greeted him with enthusiasm.

Fisher sang, joked and talked about his life since becoming a soldier. His experiences differed from ours, but we laughed in all the right places. He told us that his favorite gigs were at the WAC units or with the nurses at MASH facilities. Much better scenery than he was looking at now, he teased.

We knew that as long as he was entertaining units along the 38th parallel, he faced the same dangers we did. That became apparent when, during his show, three incoming artillery rounds burst a few hundred yards up the hillside just behind us.

"Guess they don't like my singing," he said as bits of shrapnel whizzed overhead. Those of us sitting on our helmets quickly slid them over our helmet liners and applauded his bravado.

Fisher and his band played the full hour, then headed back to Seoul. Their visit was a reminder of home and a welcome break for our battalions before we headed back to our duties.

The only improvement might have been to include one of the beautiful females Fisher later married. Debbie Reynolds or Elizabeth Taylor—either would have been OK.

JACK HICKEY · SPRING, TX

FRIENDS FOR LIFE

I WENT TO COLLEGE ON THE GI BILL
after serving in the Korean War. Because
I was a veteran, I did not have to live in a
freshman dormitory at Stout State College
(now the University of Wisconsin-Stout)
in Menomonie. Instead, I rented a room
in the south end of town.

On a walk to the campus one morning,
I bumped into Bill Hemsey, who was
unhappy with the boardinghouse where
he lived. I told him that our boardinghouse
had two vacant rooms, so he moved. Not
long after that, a friend of Bill's named
Jim Cain moved in.

We were all amiable, clean-cut guys
who quickly became lifelong friends,
corresponding every Christmas. I was
Bill's best man in 1957 and he was mine
in 1959. We were the modern version
of the Three Musketeers.

BRUCE KING · HAMILTON, MT

The Three Musketeers (from left),
Bruce, Jim and Bill, toast each
other with Bireley's soda while
studying one Saturday evening.

A GAMBLE ON KINDNESS
My older brother Nick got drafted
at 21, a year after the Korean War
began. While stationed in Linz,
Austria, he observed a craps game
among a group of soldiers one night.
A heavyset master sergeant didn't
have enough money to call the bet.
Out of the blue, Nick handed him
the cash. The sergeant won the pot.

Turns out the sergeant was
a top man in personnel. Nick was
transferred to Leghorn, also known
as Livorno, on the coast in sunny Italy,
where he lived in a hotel for six
months until some billets were built.

I was later stationed in France,
but I always chided Nick for spending
the Korean War in an Italian hotel.
MICHAEL AUGUSTA
MATAWAN, NJ

SPEEDING TO KOREA
I enlisted in the Army Security
Agency in December 1951 with the
Korean War in full swing. I reported to
Fort Devens, in Massachusetts, where
my sergeant's first order was to write
a letter home advising my parents
to sell the outside toilet because
my backside now belonged to him.

After many weeks of ASA
schooling, my squad received our
orders to report to the Far East. Five
of us jumped into a car and began
our last trip home to Pennsylvania
for a two-week furlough. Naturally,
the speed limit was not on our
minds—until we heard a siren.
A state police officer pulled us
over and approached the window.

"Where are you going?" he asked.

"To Korea," I answered.

The cop took a look at our
uniforms and chewed on it for
a minute. "Keep it under 50 here
in Connecticut," he finally said.
"Speed all you want in New York
and Pennsylvania."
ARTHUR F. STORTZ
EMMAUS, PA

Cold War Incident

On a brisk winter day in 1952, Eddy Johnson and I took the train to Hamburg, Germany, on a three-day pass from our Air Force unit in Bremerhaven, on the North Sea.

Eddy and I were corporals and were required to wear uniforms off base. At age 20 and looking for a good time, we went to the famous Reeperbahn, an area much like Times Square in New York City, with nightclubs, bars and other entertainment.

We strolled the entire length of the area, conspicuous in our uniforms. We passed a side street where a woman stood near a taxi and driver. She called to us and we approached. She was pleasant and friendly and spoke excellent English. She offered to take us around Hamburg; it would cost us nothing.

Eddy immediately said "no thanks." However, I persuaded him to take up her offer. So the four of us got into the taxi and away we went. She took us to a famous club. We had fun until she asked what we did. We both were radio intercept operators—highly classified work, with top-secret clearances. But we couldn't tell her that. We had to be careful; this was the Cold War.

Eddy told her we were truck drivers. "Not with those hands you don't drive trucks," she said.

"We drive clean trucks," he replied.

As we arrived at our first stop, I was getting leery, but determined to play it out. We entered a crowded club filled with smoke. The woman ordered us special drinks and when they came, I directed the waiter to our companion for payment.

She and the waiter spoke a foreign language. Never was any money passed, nor was there a scene. We decided not to finish our drinks and told the woman we wanted to leave. She agreed, and still no money passed hands.

We went to the next club, where we ordered beer, and again no money exchanged hands. I asked the woman to return us to the Reeperbahn. She seemed disappointed but agreed.

Days later, Eddy and I discussed our night in Hamburg, both of us having read about a town in Russia where they trained intelligence agents. The place was set up to look like a typical American town, with motels, churches, restaurants, even movies. We decided that our mystery tour guide must have been a Russian agent and that we should report her.

When we finished our story, the first sergeant said, "I don't believe you," and walked out of his office. We never solved the mystery.

RUSSELL N. COLLINS · UMATILLA, FL

Cpls. Eddy Johnson and Russell Collins sport wooden shoes and pipes during their adventures in Europe in 1952.

Holding the diver's helmet here, Kenny proudly served his community.

After attending night school, Kenny was appointed assistant fire chief in Moses Lake.

ONE IF BY LAND, TWO IF BY SEA

AFTER SERVING HIS COUNTRY IN the Navy during the early 1950s, my late father-in-law, Kenny Montgomery, returned to his home in Moses Lake, Washington, and became a firefighter. My husband loves to tell the story about the time he and his friends set a vacant lot on fire while playing with matches, only to have his father arrive to put it out.

Back then, as now, firefighters had a responsibility to the whole community. Not only did Kenny's unit fight fires, but it also performed search-and-rescue

missions on land and water. Throughout the year, the firefighters took part in the town's parades and celebrations.

Kenny later became the fire chief of newly incorporated Lynnwood, Washington. He said the hardest time he had on the job was the day he had to carry a child who hadn't made it out of a burning home. The nightmares of that day lasted his lifetime, he said.

Kenny died of lung cancer but not before leaving a lasting impression of what it means to be a hero. He may be gone, but he is not forgotten.

DIANE KAZALA
GILBERT, AZ

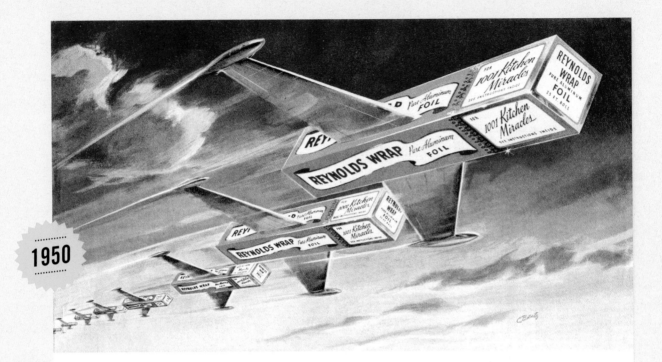

Return Flight Guaranteed!

Here, flying away by Government order, is Reynolds Wrap...
the pure aluminum foil that kept leftovers fresh, covered
bowls so neatly and quickly, made roasting and baking so much
easier and better. Aluminum foil is needed by the armed
forces ... to protect rations, medical supplies, rustable parts
and delicate instruments.

This protection is the more important because our
supply lines are long, and because they must extend to whatever
future fronts the defense of Freedom may require. The amount
of aluminum used as "fighting foil" is small compared to the
tons of aluminum in planes, ships, tanks, trucks, pontoon
bridges, bazooka and other rocket tubes. But a first aid packet
can be as vital as any weapon; all these needs have the
same urgent priority.

For all this, and to restore civilian supply as soon as
possible, the U. S. aluminum industry is rapidly expanding
production. We face a double job: fighting shortages and
inflation while we fight aggression. Reynolds is working
at that double job *full time, full speed!*
Reynolds Metals Company, General Sales Offices, Louisville 1, Ky.

Reynolds Wrap is now
"all out" for defense

Return Flight
Guaranteed!

REYNOLDS ALUMINUM

REYNOLDS WRAP aluminum foil had many important uses outside of the
kitchen for troops overseas in the '50s. According to this ad, it protected
medical supplies, rustable parts and delicate instruments. It was "fighting foil"
that was "all out" for defense. Production was expected to expand at the time.

AN OVERDUE REUNION WITH THE PAST

Returning to a South Korea he'd seen ravaged by war 50 years earlier, FRANK NICOLAZZO of Rochester, New York, was greeted with warmth, acts of generosity and a sense of the country's gratitude for all veterans. He shared photos showing more than half a century of memories.

....

1. Frank and Judith married a week before he left for Korea. **2.** On a troop train heading north, Frank doled out rations. **3.** Frank's view of a devastated Korea when he arrived in 1952. **4.** After the war, Seoul transformed into a thriving metropolis. **5.** Veterans were honored during Frank's visit to Korea. **6.** Frank returned to Korea for the 50th and 60th memorials.

DRUMMING A NEW TUNE

In 1953, I was an Army private on my way to Alaska from Fort Lewis, Washington.

We boarded a troop ship on Thanksgiving Day, where our holiday meal was a plate of Navy pork and beans. There were several 55-gallon metal container drums scattered about the ship. I wondered how we soldiers could make enough trash to fill them. The next day, in the middle of the Pacific Ocean, I realized their true purpose.

Up and down went the ship, rolling to both sides; the food wouldn't stay down. Hundreds of us made use of those handy metal bins. On deck, we used the ocean instead of the container drums.

It was a miserable few days. I was glad to get off in Alaska instead of having to retch all the way to Japan.
CHARLES GARRETT
FORT GAINES, GA

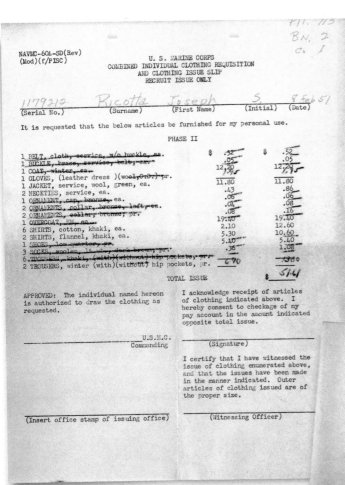

THE BOTTOM LINE IN 1951

What is Korea? Where is Korea? That's what the students from my high school graduating class in Falconer, New York, were saying.

I graduated in June 1950. In January 1951, I enlisted in the Marines. All who entered the Marine Corps had to take boot training (14 weeks at Parris Island for me).

This is the price list (left) of my first clothing issue. As you can see, it cost Uncle Sam $51.61 to dress a recruit in 1951. I also found the list (below) of items I got from the supply shed in 1953.

I thought there might be an old jarhead somewhere who would get a chuckle from these records.
JOSEPH RICOTTA · BEVERLY HILLS, FL

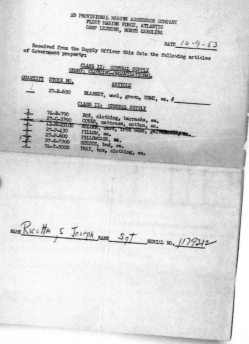

In 1951, Uncle Sam valued a Marine's winter trousers with hip pockets at $6.90 (above). In 1953, all bedding, from sheets to the pillow, was itemized (right), possibly in triplicate.

Alaska and Hawaii became states in the same year, 1959.

FROM BOYHOOD GAMES TO THE REAL WORLD

THE '50s BEGAN FOR ME AS A TIME OF innocence and ended in a time of reality.

We played ball, went sledding, climbed trees, swam in the ponds and threw rocks down the mine shafts to see how deep they were. We rode our bicycles to the creek to hang out. We stayed out until dark and our parents never worried.

Then I went to high school, and things changed. I rode around in friends' cars or borrowed Dad's car to go on dates with my girl. I worked in a grocery store for a year after I graduated in 1957, and then I joined the Marine Corps.

Reality set in; the fun and games were over. I was stationed at the Marine Corps Air Station at Kaneohe Bay, Territory Hawaii, on Aug. 21, 1959, when Hawaii officially became our 50th state.

It was a decade to remember and a reminder of how our lives change with time.

KEITH BROWN • JOPLIN, MO

NOT WHAT HE WAS TRAINED FOR

After graduating in 1951 from Wilby High School in Waterbury, Connecticut, I enlisted in the Army. I had 16 weeks of infantry training at Fort Dix, New Jersey, then went to Fort Benning, Georgia, for airborne (parachute) training. Next, after receiving my jump wings, I was transferred to Fort Bragg, North Carolina, where I received orders for combat duty in Korea.

At the end of the war, my unit moved to Camp Wood, near Kumamoto, Japan. I had never driven a car and had no driver's license, but that didn't matter to the Army—they assigned me to the motor pool. My duties were to maintain a jeep and keep it ready for inspection.

One Saturday, a motor-pool inspection was called and I stood proudly beside my jeep. The commanding general stopped in front of me and asked, "Son, how often do you change this vehicle's oil?" With my chest puffed out, I said, "Once a day, sir." Naturally, my sergeant was unhappy with that answer. He ordered me to memorize the jeep's manual.

Still, I have many fond memories of the Army. It made a man out of me.

RICHARD E. MEEHAN • FLOWERY BRANCH, GA

Floyd's platoon went to Fuji, Japan, to join the Third Marine Division on its way to Korea.

Out to Sea

Soft voices across the water resonated with meaning.

With the war raging in Korea, I joined the Marine Corps in May 1951. Two months later I was called to active duty and sent to the Marine Corps Recruit Depot (MCRD) in San Diego, California. A tenuous truce was called later that month, and the peace talks at Panmunjom began. Few of us believed the truce would last.

I was assigned to Platoon 209, billeted in Quonset huts on the north side of the grounds. In the huts to our immediate west, another platoon was formed of members who were Chinese, Japanese, Filipino and Hawaiian, but no one of European descent.

They were a good group of soldiers. I suspect they'd had some training before arriving because they were skilled at marching and handling weapons, and from the beginning they particularly excelled at discipline. One thing stood out in this platoon: They sang as they marched. And they were incredibly good. Imagine 52 soldiers marching along singing in perfect harmony. They sang native Hawaiian songs and popular songs equally well.

That platoon went with us from boot camp to our advance combat training at Camp Pendleton (near San Diego) to cold-weather training in the Sierras and finally back to Camp Pendleton for the staging regiment, the last step before being sent overseas.

The peace talks were foundering, and the truce hung by a thread that could be broken by an accidental shot or the wrong words at the peace table.

On the eve of Dec. 7, we were trucked to the Naval Shipyard in San Diego and loaded aboard an MSTS (Military Sea Transportation Service) vessel, the USNS *Gordon*. Without a doubt,

"Now is the hour that we must say goodbye. Soon we'll be sailing, far across the sea. While I'm away, oh then remember me."

at 623 feet long, this was the biggest ship I had ever seen afloat.

Blackout conditions were in force, so no lights were allowed. Marines gathered on the deck, anywhere there was room. Voices were hushed as we awaited the inevitable. Finally, in the black of night, tugs pushed us away from the dock. Powerful rumbling told us the ship was coming to life. The *Gordon* was moving under its own power.

From the darkness of the ship we could see the lights of San Diego to the north, the naval shipyards nearby, and the MCRD to the south. The lights formed a semicircle, and the *Gordon* moved toward the coal black horizon and the open sea. As we came closer to the mouth of the harbor, the soft voices of the singing platoon rose from the fantail of the ship.

The sound still rings in my ears: "Now is the hour that we must say goodbye. Soon we'll be sailing, far across the sea. While I'm away, oh then remember me."

FLOYD D. NORSKOG · KANAB, UT

When John Wayne Came to Town

In the early '50s, my husband, Ralph Dufour, was stationed at Camp Pendleton outside San Diego, California. During that time, the movie *Flying Leathernecks* was being filmed there, and some of the Marines were asked to be extras. That's how we met the film's star, John Wayne. He couldn't have been nicer to the young Marines, as you can tell from this photo of him posing with Ralph.
ANN DUFOUR · MOLINE, IL

MORE AND MORE families took recreational road trips across America in the 1950s exploring our nation's national parks. This family camps by a lake in scenic Rocky Mountain National Park in 1959.

MOTORING MEMORIES

Whether it was on a cross-country trip or a ride to the local drive-in, America fell in love with cars.

DRIVE-IN MOVIES

On June 6, 1933, the first drive-in movie theater opened in Camden, New Jersey. It charged 25 cents per car and 25 cents per person. Soon, drive-ins spread throughout the country, the number reaching some 4,000 in the '50s and '60s. They tended to show B movies, but if you were a teenager on a date, who cared what was playing?

CALLING NEAL!

When I was in high school in San Augustine, Texas, the drive-in movie theater, fondly referred to as the passion pit, was about the only place to take a date in our small town. My Uncle Ed owned the Edgewood Drive-in Theater, and we had a gentleman's agreement—he would let my date and me in for free, but I had to work the snack bar during intermission. My cue was a deep voice coming over the speakers: "Neal, come to the snack bar!" When I took my future wife on our first date, in 1956, it was at the Edgewood. Right before intermission, that deep voice intoned, "Neal, come to the snack bar!" It startled her, to say the least, especially when I had to leave her for 20 minutes to work off my debt.

NEAL MURPHY
SAN AUGUSTINE, TX

HE PROPOSED

It was May 1957. I was parked at the drive-in with my boyfriend of seven months, giggling madly about all the things that had gone wrong for me that day. After several minutes, he flat-out asked, "Are you going to be silly all evening?"

"Why?" I asked.

"Because I want to ask you to be my wife."

Please don't ask me what movie was playing that night; I was too excited to notice.

MONA HOBSON · UNION, OH

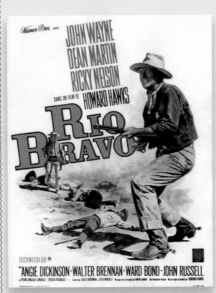

FINALLY SAW *RIO BRAVO*

In 1959, my girlfriends and I went to the Vermont Drive-in, in Torrance, California, to see *Rio Bravo*. Why? Because Ricky Nelson was in the movie, and who wasn't in love with Ricky? Once we were inside, four young men parked next to us and chatted us up. What could we do? We rolled down our windows and chatted back. We never did watch the movie—we were too busy yakking. I began dating one of the boys. The next year, we were married, and still are, some 55 years later. Recently, my sister gave us a DVD of the movie. After all these years, I finally got to see *Rio Bravo*!

SANDI FORSBERG
COARSEGOLD, CA

IXNAY

When my husband and I were dating, we often went to the drive-in to steal a kiss or two. One night, he sat stiffly and wouldn't touch me. "What's the matter?" I asked.

"See that car in front of us?" he asked.

"Yes."

"My parents are in it."

'Nough said.

LINDA HAZELWOOD
PORTERVILLE, CA

EVERYTHING JUST RIGHT

Mom popped pans of popcorn and loaded it into a brown paper grocery bag. Dad filled up his hammered aluminum Coleman cooler with ice and Pepsis, and off we went to the drive-in, my brother and I dressed in our pajamas. We'd try out a few different spots, looking for one with a good working speaker. Once we'd parked, my brother and I ran off to the playground under the screen and played with all the other kids in their pajamas until it was dark and the movie began. Dad rolled the window down on our old Ford station wagon, and my brother and I sat on the roof with our bowls of popcorn and bottles of Pepsi. Best seat in the house!

JULIE WOELTJE
VIA FACEBOOK

ON THE RUN

Once, when the movies were over, it started raining quite heavily. We bolted out of there, taking the speakers with us! We didn't mean to—we just forgot to unhook them from the windows. I was so scared, but nothing ever happened. It was quite a while before we returned to that drive-in.

PEGGY McKENZIE
VIA FACEBOOK

Bouldin and his wife, Clarice, stand in front of his cool redo of a 1956 Plymouth Fury.

Revival Meeting

Careful rebuild brings back cool memories—but without air conditioning.

When I was in college, I owned a car like the 1956 Plymouth Fury above. I have asked myself over and over why I got rid of it, and have concluded that I was just too dumb to appreciate what I had. My son, who got tired of hearing me bellyache about it, found this one in Ohio. Our off-the-frame restoration took four years.

My original car had a push-button transmission, power steering, power brakes, power windows and factory air conditioning, a very rare option back then. The air-conditioning evaporator took up the entire rear deck in the trunk, and the vents came up through the rear hat shelf, with deflectors to prevent cold air from blowing on passengers' heads in the backseat. This car has all the accessories of my original except for the air conditioning.

For this model, you could specify whatever color you wanted as long as it was eggshell white. The gold top was not stock, but since my original car had a gold top, we decided to paint this one the same way. The side panels and wheel covers are stock gold-anodized aluminum.

The coupes came equipped with a 240-horsepower, 303-cubic-inch V-8 built in Canada, a heavy-duty suspension and a beefed-up powertrain. Because this one didn't have an engine when we bought it, my son installed a 392-cubic-inch Hemi. We couldn't adapt the push buttons (which are still installed) to the new transmission, so we settled for a floor shifter.

The redone Fury brings back fond memories of my first car. Clarice and I dated in it and, for our honeymoon, took it from Atlanta, Georgia, where I was in school, to New Orleans, Louisiana. I drove it for 80,000 trouble-free miles.

We've driven the new car only a few hundred miles so far, but we look forward to many more. It's fun to watch people react to it—many have never seen this model before.

BOULDIN FRANTZ · ROANOKE, VA

THE LITTLE AUTO THAT COULD

WHEN I WAS A CHILD, my parents owned one of America's smallest cars. It was a 1952 Crosley Super Station Wagon—a FINE car, as it read in the ads. My mother took this photo of me (below) beside the Lilliputian auto in 1954.

I was only a foot shorter than the roof. The tires were a mere 12 inches smaller than the wheels on my brother's Schwinn. On the back of one photo, Mum had written "Mary's Clown Car." Family and friends enjoyed teasing my short, red-haired mother as she loaded the Crosley with kids and groceries to the ceiling.

The two-door pixie wagon was blue with wood-weave decal panels.

The interior was gray with red imitation-leather seats, a small back bench and a single rear door.

It seemed as if Mum went through a checklist to get the car started. Choke, start, clutch, shift and off we'd go. Mum transported me and my two siblings around our hometown of Framingham, Massachusetts. Then there were the extended journeys to our summer cottage at Sebago Lake, Maine. The 150-mile jaunt took all day driving along the coast road. I'd ask Mum, "Can't you go faster?"

She'd reply, "This is a small car; you have to be patient."

When my sister Shirley and her girlfriends traveled the back roads, every bump would send their heads into the ceiling. Instead of slowing when she saw a dip ahead, she'd yell, "Duck!"

One year, Dad spruced up the car for Mum. He had the Crosley painted to match his 1955 Ford wagon colors of aqua and white. For fun, he also had a Bermuda bell mounted under the floor. It was shaped like an upturned bowl, with a loud ding-dong tone, rung by a plunger operated by foot.

Even today, that little car inspires some larger-than-life memories of my family.

DEBBIE McNAUGHTON
SOUTH YARMOUTH, MA

Debbie seems about the right size for the 1952 Crosley Super Station Wagon.

The front and back ends of the 1958 MG Magnette sedan certainly were sharp-looking. The dash was made of old English wood.

A Spot of Buzzy Cool from Across the Pond

The MG Magnette sedan was marketed to the young urban professional in England in the 1950s. I could remember seeing only a couple of these even in the '50s. Today, there may be fewer than 200 of the cars in North America.

I spotted my 1958 Magnette in the used-car ads in a newspaper in 1999. I'd owned an MG of a different model years before. I had really liked that car, so I figured I definitely needed this one. I bought the Magnette and drove it home; at 55 mph it sure sounded like the model I used to own.

When I got it home and started sorting it out, I was pleased to find that the engine was very familiar—the only problem being, it was regurgitating large puddles of oil onto my garage floor. That was quickly remedied when I discovered that the valve cover gasket had a kink in it.

I liked tinkering with the engine, but the twin SU side-draft carburetors were tricky to synchronize. The body had no dents or rust. The only parts that were really worn were the carpet, the seats and the weather stripping. I found the weather stripping locally, put some covers on the seats and cut new carpet using the old one as a pattern. I did have the car repainted, but the original paint wasn't bad. I wish I'd left it alone.

The dash and the wood trim were honest-to-goodness old English wood. I rubbed Old English Lemon Oil on them. The old door panels perked up with Armor All.

With the 4:10 rear end and the four-speed floor shifter linked up to the 1.5-liter four-cylinder engine, first gear would get you about half the way across an intersection. At 66 mph on the highway it sounded and felt as if the car was doing 99. This model, refreshed in 1956, got an engine upgrade to 68 horsepower, which raised the top speed to 86. I never got it up to 86 mph, but if I had, it probably would have sounded as if it was going to go airborne. At 65 mph, I couldn't hear myself think in there.

I enjoyed the MG for three or four years. Then I got tired of scraping ice off my Subaru's windows out in the driveway in winter while the vintage car sat snug and dry in the garage. I sold it to a retired mechanical engineer who lived on Long Island in New York.

MIKE CASEY · AURORA, CO

A BELOVED SEDAN FROM A FAVORITE MAKER

I'VE BEEN A CAR GUY most of my life. It began in 1952 when my uncle, who was a lance corporal in the Marines, sold his Studebaker sedan to my dad. My uncle was going to wartime South Korea on indefinite assignment. That sedan became our family's primary transportation until 1959; later, Studebaker became my favorite make of automobile. I have a vivid memory of mastering the three-speed shift on the steering column with the coordinating clutch/gas-pedal movement.

In 1990, I bought this 1957 Studebaker President sedan from a World War II veteran who had acquired it in an estate sale. The car was originally dark green but now sported new teal blue paint. The upholstery was floral blue, and on the dashboard was the maker's Cyclops Eye speedometer, which changed color as the speed increased. It had power steering and a 289-cubic-inch V8 engine that was mated to an automatic transmission.

I did find a gremlin: The battery kept going dead. Eventually I located a dome light wire that was touching the roof metal and shorting the battery out.

I went to all the local car shows in my area of Maryland. I never tried to win a trophy, but a lot of people got to know my car. Many people would misidentify it until they walked around to the trunk to read the manufacturer's name.

I drove the car around for about 10 years until I wore it out. A mechanic told me that the cost to restore it would be prohibitive, so I decided to give it up. I'm fortunate to have a lot of pictures to remind me of its glory days.

EDWARD LEMANSKI
JESSUP, MD

Edward's beloved 1957 Studebaker President is truly missed.

ROADTRIP OF A LIFETIME

Three buddies from Pearl River, New York—from left, Bill, **JOHN D. BAKER** and Butch—headed to California in June 1950, a year before joining the military. They drove 72 hours straight in a 1936 Ford convertible on their way to Needles, California, and saw just about everything on Route 66. "I would do it all again today if I could," John writes from Sebastian, Florida.

MOTOR MOUTH

To be considered king of the road, your street talk has to be up to snuff. Here's a lingo lesson:

Agitate the gravel: To leave

Burn rubber or peel out: Leave tire marks

Chariot: Car

Deuce: 1932 Ford

Flip-top or ragtop: Convertible

Go for pinks: Race for pink slip or ownership papers

Hottie: Very fast car

Jacked up: Describing a car with a raised rear end

Souped up: Modified for speed

Stack up: Wreck a car

Tank: A large sedan

Wail: Go fast

"IT LOOKS LIKE A THUNDERBIRD!"

As young newlyweds in 1958, we had high hopes of owning our first house, starting a family and having a bright future together. We needed a car and favored a late-model Ford Thunderbird, but on our tight budget, it was an impossible dream. Then we read an automotive magazine article describing a new import from England, the Sunbeam Alpine.

We visited a dealer and agreed it was close to our ideal automobile (and affordable!). It had red leather seats, wire knock-off wheels like those on racing cars, and a hard top with rounded side windows, which could be replaced in the summer with a convertible soft top and tonneau cover. It was our pride and joy until 1963, when we traded it in for a Ford Country Squire station wagon to accommodate our new baby accessories!

BOB AND HELENE BECHER • MYRTLE BEACH, SC

Helene Becher (above) poses in the Sunbeam Alpine. We dig those stylish sunglasses, too, Helene!

The hardtop version of the Nash Rambler Country Club debuted in 1951.

JUST LIKE IN HIGH SCHOOL

I GREW UP ON A WISCONSIN DAIRY FARM IN the 1950s, and from an early age, I drove tractors and trucks all around the farm. My dad could fix almost anything, and he taught me basic car mechanics.

I went on to a military and civil service career of more than 40 years, and while I did do a few car restorations during that period, retirement allowed me to devote more time to my hobby.

I decided to look for a car similar to the one I'd had in high school, a 1951 Nash Rambler Country Club. It was not a mainstream model—approximately 19,000 were built.

After three years of looking, I found one in Salt Lake City, Utah. Although I live in Illinois and was nervous to buy it sight unseen, I was afraid it would take too long to find another. Nonetheless, I was pleased with the car's condition when it arrived.

In the last four years, I have rebuilt most of its mechanical systems, including the engine.

I had a friend do the bodywork and paint in the original color scheme. Had the interior not already been restored to those colors, I would have done it in the color of my high school car—baby blue!

MIKE KLEPP · OAKWOOD, IL

STARS, CIGARS AND CARS AT THE INDY SPEEDWAY

Back in 1950, I won four tickets to the Indianapolis 500 through a local radio station. Two of the tickets were for the press box, and the other two were for seats by the starting line.

As my dad and I walked through the tunnel to the press box, we had to step aside to allow movie stars Clark Gable and Barbara Stanwyck to pass by. They were at the race filming the movie *To Please a Lady.*

The press box was packed with men sitting behind rows of typewriters, and the room was choked with smoke from the reporters' cigars.

I remember the excitement building as we walked to the track for the start of the race.

All 33 cars were lined up as "Back Home Again in Indiana" and then "The Star-Spangled Banner" played over the loudspeaker.

Then came the famous words "Gentlemen, start your engines."

The sky filled with red, white and blue balloons, the green flag dropped, and the race was on.

Sadly, as the day wore on, clouds moved in and then rain. The race was eventually halted at 345 miles. But Dad and I had had a great time anyway.

MARLYN "BUD" WHITE WILTON, IA

This press pin is a memento of Marlyn's trip to the Indy 500.

CARS

Vintage Ads

Come on, let's go for a ride! The American auto industry in the 1950s got creative with car offerings for an eager public.

YOUR SHELL DEALER GETS UNDER YOUR CAR'S HOOD AND CHECKS YOUR OIL

Incomparable!

SHELL X-100 MOTOR OIL

SHELL

Corrosive Acid Action—not friction—causes up to 90% of engine wear. Millions of miles of use by motorists have proved that Shell X-100 Motor Oil counteracts acid action—prolongs engine life.

YOUR OIL CHANGE TIME IS DETERMINED BY MANY THINGS—WEATHER—MILEAGE AND THE WAY YOU DRIVE

EVERY TIME YOU DRIVE INTO HIS STATION—WHEN HE SAYS "BETTER CHANGE" HE MEANS SHELL X-100

DRAIN-FLUSH AND REFILL YOUR CRANKCASE NOW WITH SHELL X-100 MOTOR OIL

1951

THROWBACK ALERT: Recently, Shell X-100 Motor Oils were reintroduced in North America for owners of classic cars with older engines. We hope Shell kept the vintage-can design that is displayed in this advertisement!

Winning combination of 1953

HERE they are — the 1953 leaders in their fields—Chevrolet, Pontiac, Oldsmobile, Buick and Cadillac.

We have photographed them against the background of the great new General Motors Technical Center near Detroit, for very good reason.

This Technical Center is the latest example of the lengths we at General Motors

go to provide our engineers with the resources to design ever-better cars for you.

In performance, in riding comfort, in driving ease, and in styling — these are, we believe, the finest cars we have ever brought to market.

Tangible proof of what GM engineering has contributed to this progress is found

in higher-compression engines and improved automatic drives, and in such special new advances as power steering, power brakes and air conditioning.

We invite you to view them at your General Motors dealers'. There is no surer way to find out for yourself that the key to a General Motors car is your key to greater value.

GENERAL MOTORS

"More and Better Things for More People"

CHEVROLET • PONTIAC
OLDSMOBILE • BUICK
CADILLAC
All with Body by Fisher
GMC TRUCK & COACH

BUICK

CADILLAC

1953

GENERAL MOTORS shows off its Buick and Cadillac models against the background of the then-new General Motors Technical Center near Detroit, Michigan.

1951 Kaiser

Now... America's
newest 2-door sedan

THE WHOLE family can fit into this spacious 1951 Kaiser DeLuxe two-door sedan featuring a split windshield with "no blind spots" and extra luggage space in the trunk.

The 1951 Kaiser DeLuxe 2-door Sedan... one of 6 body styles and 12 models. Hydra-Matic Drive available in all models at extra cost.

Control-Tower Vision...The largest windshield in any car (1096 square inches), with the slimmest, slant-back corner posts, lets you see all around... no "blind spots"! That's how Anatomic Design considers your eyes!

Extra Luggage Space...cleaner, clearer, because the spare tire is in a Tuck-Away Tire Well under trunk compartment, not in it! There's more passenger space, too... wider seats, greater head and leg room. Anatomic Design considers your size!

Lower Center of Gravity...yet there's full road clearance! Hugs the roads closer, safer—even on the sharpest curves! Over-sized jumbo brakes assure swifter, softer stopping. That's the way Anatomic Design considers your peace of mind!

Supersonic Power...The new 115 h.p. Kaiser Supersonic High-Torque Engine gives you faster acceleration, instant obedience, and smoother, quieter power that saves you money every mile that you drive! Yes, Anatomic Design considers your pocketbook, too!

Built to Better the Best on the Road

Triumph of

Anatomic Design*

*The newest, most advanced step in motor car making. It is the technique of styling and engineering every feature of the body and chassis to serve the needs of the human anatomy. The result ... se of handling

...'s the newest car in America

...you'll want to <u>own</u> it

© 1950 KAISER-FRAZER SALES CORP., WILLOW RUN, MICHIGAN

THE SATURDAY EVENING POST
February 10, 1951

Dollar for Dollar you can't beat a
Pontiac

All it needs is <u>you</u> behind the wheel!

PONTIAC MOTOR DIVISION OF GENERAL MOTORS CORPORATION

THE SLEEK beauty of a blue Pontiac is showcased in this simple and direct ad personifying the car. Indeed, then as now, customers saw their vehicles as extensions of themselves and their personalities.

A spring ad campaign announced "The Edsel is Coming" five months before the car's release. Once unveiled, the vehicle got a lot of lookers; buyers, not so much.

THIS FAILURE CAME WITH A PERK

Test-drive the car; leave with a mini version.

SIXTY YEARS AGO, THE FORD MOTOR CO. introduced its ill-fated Edsel with all the suspense of an Alfred Hitchcock movie. Ads promised "a new vista of motoring pleasure, unlike any other car you've ever seen." To heighten anticipation, the cars were hidden under tarps during transport, and showroom windows were papered over until "E Day." It worked. People lined up to see the new Edsel when it was unveiled, on Sept. 4, 1957.

To keep showroom traffic flowing afterward, Ford launched a volley of newspaper ads, postcards and promotional fliers touting, "Road-check the big one, get a little one free."

The giveaway featured gift boxes holding ⅟₂₅-scale promotional models, or promos, with durable plastic bodies, metal chassis and moving wheels.

LUKE MILLER · URBANDALE, IA

Toying with Car Buyers– and Their Kids

As president of the Florida Edsel Club and a collector of Edsel promos, I can honestly say the toys Ford distributed had a dual purpose. Number one, they kept kids quiet so the salesmen could hold parents' attention. Number two, they built brand awareness in kids so that later, when they grew up to be customers, they'd remember the toys they played with as youngsters.

Just one color and body style—a turquoise-and-white coupe—was used in the campaign. But dealers kept promos in other body styles and colors on hand. These were useful for showing customers what the cars would look like in different colors, especially in rural locations where all the options might not be available for easy viewing.

I should know. In the late 1950s, my father, Emil Cerame, was a Mercury-Edsel-Lincoln dealer in my rural hometown of Avon, New York. He kept promotional models in the dealership. And at the end of the model year, he'd give the leftovers to the Little League team he sponsored.

As toys, most promos were eventually broken and discarded, increasing the value of surviving cars. Today, they're popular with toy collectors and Edsel owners alike.

I suppose there are buyers as well who want an Edsel but can't afford one, so the model is the next best thing.

ROB CERAME · DAYTONA BEACH, FL

WHAT'S THAT EDSEL PROMO WORTH TODAY?

Edsel dealers used turquoise-and-white promos in the test-drive giveaway. Aluminum Model Toys Inc. (AMT), a toy manufacturer, made Edsel promos in a variety of factory colors for dealer use but switched up color combinations or treatments on cars sold in toy stores.

....

AMT built convertible and two-door hardtop promos for all three Edsel model years: 1958, 1959 (shown here) and 1960.

....

Today, the 1960 Edsel promos can run more than $100 apiece.

....

An average-condition turquoise 1958 coupe, the most common, can garner $30 to $35; other colors bring around $60.

....

Promotional models in unusual colors can bring $300 to $400.

FILLED WITH FUN

Our cousins Jerry and Artis Phillips grew up near my brothers and me west of Lake Worth, Texas. Their dad owned a small gas station—sized just right for kids to play around the pumps—on the Jacksboro Highway.

Folks who pulled into the station would shout, "Fill 'er up!" and they'd also expect to have the windshield washed and the air in the tires checked, free of charge. Bigger stations might give away toys, calendars or even road maps. I remember going to an Exxon station and getting a tiger's tail as a reminder to "put a tiger in your tank."

After a long day of playing, we'd reach inside a bin of ice-cold sodas for a frosty RC Cola, Orange Crush or my favorite, Grapette.

MARY TATUM TAYLOR · IRVING, TX

Mary's cousin Jerry Phillips (left) and brother John Tatum as young pump jockeys in the 1950s.

DO YOU WANT FRIES WITH THAT?

Back in the summer of 1950, four of us 20-year-olds drove out to explore the national parks. In Yellowstone, we'd see bears roaming the roads, looking for food. One of their tricks was to stand against the side of a car and beg for a handout through the window. I snapped this picture as a bear leaned into the backseat of my Plymouth. It almost looks like a carhop taking an order at a drive-in.

HOWARD JOHNSON · ZEELAND, MI

RAINY DAY DRUTHERS

I sold a 1951 Plymouth convertible for about $200 in 1957 to a man for his college-bound daughter. A year later, he asked me to sell the car for him. I told him he could sell it himself, but he insisted that I do it. I told him that whatever I sold it for, I would keep half, and he agreed. He also said he had installed a new white convertible top.

After giving the car a tuneup, I sold it for $100 and split the money. About three weeks later, the new owner called from Albany, New York, to say he couldn't get the car started.

It was raining cats and dogs when I met him on Central Avenue. As I checked over the Plymouth, it started raining harder. So we got into the car—and I found out why the previous owner had asked me to sell it for him. The convertible top he'd installed leaked like a sieve.

The $50 I got from that sale wasn't nearly enough to pay for the embarrassment I suffered sitting in that car.

EDWARD E. HILLIGRASS
JOHNSONVILLE, NY

THE ONE THAT GOT AWAY

I was driving my dad's car through town in June 1958 when I passed a used-car lot with a beautiful Chevrolet Impala convertible parked out front. It was white with red upholstery. I bought it on the spot.

A few days later the dealer asked if I could leave the vehicle with him on Friday because there were some minor items that he had to replace. I could pick it up on Monday morning. What I didn't know was that the FBI took the car to a garage and stripped it down to check all the serial numbers.

When I went to get the car, the dealer and an FBI agent told me that it had been stolen in New York and sent to Lawrence, Massachusetts, for resale. The first car that I ever owned turned out to be someone else's! What's more, "my" car had helped the FBI to break up a five-state stolen-car ring.

The dealer apologized, and two weeks later he replaced my stolen car with a newer Chevrolet Impala convertible. It had all been quite an adventure.

LOUIS PALAZZO · SALEM, NH

Barbara's baby—a Sierra Gold 1958 Chevy Impala—first belonged to her dad, Leo. Now she enjoys taking the family's classic car out for auto shows and local parades.

Ride into the '50s

Dad's cool car took her on many adventures—and landed her in the local paper!

've always been fascinated with the 1950s. It's the decade my parents graduated from high school, got married and started their life together. It's also when my dad, Leo Stuck, bought the two-door 1958 Chevy Impala I loved so much as a child.

When my friends and I were in elementary school, we would sit in the car in the driveway, pretending we were going on a trip to Florida. One of us would be the dad, one the mom and the rest the children. Of course, we'd change roles every few minutes, because all of us wanted a chance to "drive."

When *Grease* was released in the summer of 1978, we dressed in a girlfriend's mother's clothes from the '50s and drove the Impala to the Palace Theater in Olean, New York, to see the movie. Before we left, we called the *Olean*

Times Herald newspaper and told a reporter about our plan.

A man met us in front of the theater and told me to park under the marquee showing the names of Olivia Newton-John and John Travolta. Then he took our picture. We felt like movie stars!

Dad always entered the Chevy in the Labor Day parade in nearby Rushford. I rode along with him, throwing candy to the crowd. When I had my own kids, they joined Dad on the parade route.

Sadly, Dad died in 1998. I inherited his car and have a lot of fun with it at parades and car shows. To those who knew Dad, it's still Leo's car. Several people have asked to buy it, but I would never sell such a special ride!

BARBARA WOOLSTON · BELMONT, NY

New **PACKARD!**

She's Still Got It

Sixty years ago, Marilyn Montgomery was chosen to adorn this 1953 Packard as part of a Camp Atterbury, Indiana, charity drive. Camp Atterbury has left our lives, as has the Packard, but Marilyn (now Logan) goes on and on, better than ever.
SCOTT LOGAN

LUCKY TEENAGERS on Dick Clark's *American Bandstand* really knew how to cut a rug. Folks watching at home could dance around their living rooms as hits from the era blared over their TV sets.

ROCKIN' AROUND THE CLOCK

Dick Clark, Johnnie Ray, Buddy Holly and other names resonate with the 1950s and a shift in music.

Holding On Through Shakes, Rattles and Rolls

The last card I opened on my 16th birthday in 1957 was from my boyfriend, Joe. It contained two tickets to Alan Freed's Rock 'n' Roll Show at the Paramount Theater in Brooklyn, New York.

At Flatbush and DeKalb avenues in Brooklyn, a huge line of teenagers wound around the block, waiting to buy tickets, while another, shorter line was for those with tickets. Joe and I felt a little overdressed standing with the denim-and-bobby-sox throng. He had on a suit and tie, and I wore a black-and-white polka-dot dress, with crinolines, stockings and patent heels.

Inside, we climbed four flights of stairs to the balcony and then made our way carefully down to our seats. Talk about nosebleed seats. With the pushing crowd, I pictured myself missing a step and landing flat on my face.

There were about 20 acts. Everyone who'd made a hit record that year seemed to be on the program. We saw the Platters, Buddy Holly and many other groups that night. The glitter from all the rhinestones and sequins on stage was dazzling. My favorite was Fats Domino, who belted out "Blueberry Hill" and "Ain't That a Shame." Fats must have soaked a dozen handkerchiefs during that performance.

Bill Haley and His Comets played "Shake, Rattle and Roll" and "Rock Around the Clock." When the balding Haley slid down on his knees to play a solo, girls fainted.

The foot stomping shook the balcony. Kids danced in the aisles and sang along. No one stayed seated. The house went silent only while Chuck Berry played "Maybelline," and when he was done, near hysteria ensued. Girls pulled their hair as if possessed, and bawled. I held on to Joe. He seemed to be the only thing that wasn't shaking.

The music was truly American—loud, energetic and wild. It was new, and it was ours.

JO MELE · MORAGA, CA

Alan Freed was the first to adopt the term "rock 'n' roll" to describe the music he played on his radio show in the early '50s.

Sonny Deall (left) was easily mistaken for a musician in '56.

'WE'RE NOT THE ROVER BOYS'

I WENT TO JUST ABOUT EVERY ALAN FREED ROCK 'N' ROLL show at the Paramount Theatre in Brooklyn, New York. In 1956, when I was 21, I went to the Easter show with my friend Ray. Whenever Ray and I went out together, we dressed alike—black suit, black bow tie and bright-colored shirt with bright socks to match. We got off the bus in our concert duds, and as we approached the side of the Paramount, a group of screaming teenage girls started to surround us.

Shoving us up against the building, they begged for our autographs. We tried to explain that we were not a part of the show, but one of the girls yelled to her friends, "Come on over here! It's some of the Rover Boys!"

They insisted on our autographs, so I wrote things like "To Josie, Love, Sonny," "To Maryanne, Love, Sonny," "Best Wishes to Dottie, Love, Sonny," and so on. After about half a dozen autographs, we hurried away into the crowd inside to enjoy the show.

We saw Fats Domino, the Teenagers, the Platters, the Willows, the Flamingos, the Valentines, Ruth McFadden, the Royaltones, the Cleftones, Dori Anne Gray, the Jodimars, Cindy and Lindy, Al Sears, and Sam "The Man" Taylor, and, finally, Alan Freed introduced the Rover Boys. As they started to sing "Graduation Day," Ray and I began to clap and yell and whistle—and then we laughed. We felt great that we'd been able to make all those girls so happy, thinking that they had met a couple of the Rover Boys.

Thanks, girls. Love, Sonny.

SONNY DEALL · KINSTON, NC

ON-AIR DANCE PARTY

On the night of July 11, 1951, a hard-drinking, chain-smoking, gravel-voiced disc jockey brought a groundbreaking new term to Cleveland radio. "Let's rock 'n' roll!" Alan Freed bellowed into the mic at station WJW. "It's the Alan Freed Rock 'n' Roll Party!"

Caught up in the sound of the rhythm-and-blues 78s that spun on his turntables, Freed pounded a beat on a Cleveland phone book and rang a cowbell, shouting "Go, man, go!" while the music blasted through the speakers. Freed's exuberant promotion of the phrase quickly earned R&B music a new label.

Earlier that year, the classical-music DJ met with buddy Leo Mintz, owner of the inner-city store Record Rendezvous. A longtime WJW sponsor, Mintz explained that nearly half of his R&B-buying customers were young white teens. Freed could gain a huge new late-night audience, Mintz promised, if he switched his format from "fuddy-duddy" classical to what teens everywhere were embracing.

The savvy Freed quickly adopted the instantly popular mixture of black jump blues, up-tempo swing and doo-wop ballads as the rock 'n' roll that would soon make him a teen-culture superstar.
RANDAL C. HILL
BANDON, OR

AMERICAN BANDSTAND

THREE DECADES OF ROCK 'N' ROLL

Millions of kids came of age—and learned to dance—watching chart-toppers on the music show hosted by the World's Oldest Living Teenager, Dick Clark. *American Bandstand* went national in 1957. The Regulars are seen dancing at right as Clark spins tunes.

THE MUSIC OF A GENERATION

Established artists like Nat "King" Cole, Perry Como and Louis Armstrong held their own in the '50s, but when Les Paul developed a solid-bodied Gibson electric guitar and marketed it around 1952, the music industry was forever changed.

In the middle of the decade, teenagers everywhere spun artists like Fats Domino, Chuck Berry and The King.

Elvis Presley released a dozen No. 1 hits from 1955 to 1959, including "Love Me Tender," "Heartbreak Hotel" and "Hound Dog." His hit single "Don't" and album "King Creole" came out shortly before Elvis became an Army private in 1958.

Other rock artists on the scene were the Everly Brothers with hits including "Bye Bye Love" and "Wake Up Little Susie," Jerry Lee Lewis with "Whole Lot of Shakin' Going On" and Little Richard with "Lucille."

And who could ever forget these all-the-rage ditties: "Luck Be a Lady," "A Bushel and a Peck," "Cry Me a River," "Love and Marriage," "I Walk the Line," "The Purple People Eater," "Tequila," "Papa Loves Mambo" and "Shake, Rattle and Roll."

1952 BILLBOARD'S TOP 10

1
"Blue Tango"
Leroy Anderson

2
"Wheel of Fortune"
Kay Starr

3
"Cry"
Johnnie Ray

4
"You Belong to Me"
Jo Stafford

5
"Auf Wiederseh'n, Sweetheart"
Vera Lynn

6
"Half as Much"
Rosemary Clooney

7
"Wish You Were Here"
Eddie Fisher and Hugo Winterhalter

8
"I Went to Your Wedding"
Patti Page

9
"Here in My Heart"
Al Martino

10
"Delicado"
Percy Faith

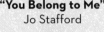

EVERETT COLLECTION

Dick Clark mans the podium as teenagers dance on his nationally televised show in Philadelphia, Pennsylvania.

Philly Teens Had the Beat

I grew up in Philly and began watching *American Bandstand* when the show was local and Bob Horn was the host, in the early '50s. I watched every day after school, learning to dance while I held onto the banister in the living room. We all wanted to be like the regulars.

I was on *Bandstand* from 1957 to 1959. My friends and I would leave school early, go to the WFIL studio and stand in line, hoping to get in. The first time I was on, I was in a teenage trance. There was Dick Clark himself!

All we wanted to do was dance. We did the jitterbug, the bunny hop, the strand, the stomp, the chalypso and more.

Philly teens set the trends for the country once *Bandstand* went national. There was a local half-hour before the national feed began, and we felt that was "our time." The music was more local, featuring doo-wop and Philly groups.

Bandstand was a must for any group that wanted exposure. Philly guys Danny and the Juniors, Frankie Avalon, Fabian, Chubby Checker, Jimmy Darren and Bobby Rydell all got started on the show.

Dick Clark knew how to work the camera and put everyone at ease. He gave teens an identity, with a show built around them.

FREDDI CARLIP
LEWISBURG, PENNSYLVANIA

BANDSTAND RATES A NATIONAL SPOT

ON MONDAY, AUG. 5, 1957, AT 3 P.M., RED CAMERA lights winked on at Philadelphia's WFIL-TV. "Hi, I'm Dick Clark," said the ageless, clean-cut 26-year-old. "Welcome to *American Bandstand*." Those eight words launched one of history's most successful national daytime television shows.

The 90-minute daily program on the ABC-TV affiliate focused on teenagers dancing to records and Clark chatting with the well-dressed audience members. (Boys wore jackets and ties; the girls, skirts or dresses.) *Bandstand* offered controlled fun. Teens evaluated new songs on Rate-a-Record, enjoyed a Spotlight Dance and learned to dance the stroll and the twist.

Musical guests often lip-synched their hits on the show, which featured a safe soundtrack of mainstream pop/rock songs that eased parents' concern over this wild and crazy new music.

Decades later, Clark recalled that now-iconic afternoon with music executive Joe Smith: "It took all of 20 minutes after we went off the air that first day for us to know we had a monster on our hands."

American Bandstand launched the careers of numerous stars.

RANDAL C. HILL
BANDON, OR

Singer Freddie "Boom Boom" Cannon holds the record for the most *American Bandstand* appearances at 110.

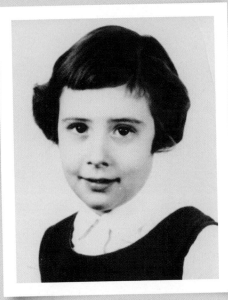

When life didn't provide a real dance buddy, Tory pressed an obliging bedpost into duty.

PINEAPPLE PARTNER

You could say Dick Clark was my first crush. I was only 6 in 1957, but my goal was to dance with Dick Clark on *American Bandstand*. Time and place meant nothing to a first-grader from New Hope, Pennsylvania—only an hour from Philadelphia, where the show was filmed. I figured I would be old enough in seven years to be a teenager in love.

I started practicing the jitterbug every day after school. But since I was an only child, I needed a stand-in boyfriend.

My parents' bed included a bedpost with a carved pineapple on top, making it a suitable height for a dance partner. The bulky 40-pound portable TV would wobble on its metal stand as I jumped and swirled nearby. But my pineapple partner never complained or criticized my dance moves.

I might have worn myself silly if it hadn't been for commercials back then, since there were no "mute" or "pause" buttons in those days. We didn't even have color TV. None of that mattered to me; Dick Clark was the most handsome star on black-and-white television.

TORY STELLABOTTE
ST. JOHNS, FL

MUSIC

Vintage Ads

Before cassettes, CDs or iPods, the best way to hear the catchiest tunes of the day was over the radio or by dropping the needle on a vinyl.

CROSLEY 1951 COLOR-STYLED RADIOS

Sound as good as they look ... and that's Wonderful !

1951

Never such smart beauty . . . such thrilling performance! Decorator-designed cabinets in striking solid colors . . . and in subtly contrasting two-tone shades. Never such variety —such versatility! You'll find *exactly* the right Crosley Radio, with precisely the right color and styling—for any room! And *inside*, even the smallest one is tone-engineered for amazing big set reception and full, rich volume! Choose Crosley — and be sure of *fine* quality, *lasting* beauty, *enduring* enjoyment!

This Christmas give a Crosley Radio. There's one for every room—purpose—occasion!

Clock Radio. In six glowing colors. Wakes you or lulls you to sleep—turns on and off automatically. Operates most electrical appliances. Series 11-120.

Richly beautiful "Coloradio." Gleaming white cabinet with chromium trim for the kitchen; five rich combinations to match color schemes in other rooms! Convenient phono connection for record player. Series 10-135.

Super-sensitive FM-AM Radio. Has great sensitivity to give you better reception of all stations. The sturdy plastic case is available in four rich simulated leather color combinations. Series 11-126.

Crosley Division (AVCO) Cincinnati 25, Ohio

Better Products for Happier Living

SHELVADOR® REFRIGERATORS • FREEZERS • ELECTRIC RANGES
STEEL KITCHEN CABINETS • SINKS • GARBAGE DISPOSERS
ELECTRIC WATER HEATERS • RADIOS • TELEVISION

"Riviera" Three-way Portable. Lift the lid and it plays; close the lid and it stops! Five appealing color schemes. It delivers truly wonderful reception on batteries, or AC-DC. Series 11-301.

Lovely "Decorator" Model. A patrician design in choice of four subtle colors. Engineered for superb console tone. Like other Crosley Radios, this beautiful set has a rich, deep bass. Series 11-106.

CROSLEY RADIOS for Christmas

PORTABLES • TABLE MODELS • CONSOLES

Compact, trim "Serenader" Radio. A great performer on office desks, night tables, end tables. Surprisingly low in price. Available in six beautiful colors. Series 11-114.

Sweet and powerful "Dynamic" Table Radio. Available in six glowing colors, with graceful lines. Provides sweet listening and a striking high spot of color for any room. Series 11-100.

YOU CAN ENJOY THE SUPERB STYLE AND PERFORMANCE OF CROSLEY RADIOS AT AMAZINGLY LOW PRICES

THE PACE-SETTING DESIGNS ARE COMING FROM CROSLEY!

TO GET your toes tapping, turn your dial back to these vintage radio designs that came in a variety of colors. One of these radios would still look terrific on display in a modern home.

Better See Motorola

FIRST IN RADIO SALES 1ST

Exclusive Golden Voice

Hi-Fidelity System

The Radio-Phonograph that brings
music lovers the answer to low-cost

Hi-Fi Tone

Motorola has done it! Discovered how to bring you radio-phonograph tone quality never before possible for less than hundreds of dollars! After years of research, Motorola now brings you all the beauty that has lain unheard in your finest records! All the highs and lows, the true, sweet treble, the full bass, the rich realism! Every record becomes a listening adventure . . . old records sound like new again! You must hear it to believe it! Ask your dealer for a demonstration of your favorite record. Hear it "for the first time!"

GOLDEN TONE ARM! Featherweight pickup, Air-tone needle and Sonogap air chamber, reduce record wear and needle noise.

FULL TONAL RANGE

FULL RADIO HOOKUP! No other record player uses full audio system of the radio. Result: wider range, greater brilliance, realism!

Motorola Hi-Fi
WORLD'S LARGEST EXCLUSIVE ELECTRONICS MANUFACTURER

MOTOROLA HI-FI RADIO-PHONOGRAPH—With 3-Speed Inter-mix Record Changer, Hi-Fi sound. 53F2, $99.95
Price subject to change without notice. Slightly higher West and South. © 1953, Motorola, Inc. "Golden Voice" is a Reg. T. M. of Motorola, Inc.

1953

THE PRICE of this Motorola Hi-Fi radio-phonograph was $99.95 in 1953, which was a low-cost option then. The ad touts that "Every record becomes a listening adventure…," as this player brings radio-phonograph tone quality.

BEFORE THE MUSIC DIED

I WAS FIRST TURNED ON TO BUDDY Holly while stationed at Fort Leonard Wood, in Missouri, and I instantly became a fan. After the Army, I attended Marquette University, in Milwaukee, Wisconsin. On Jan. 29, 1959, when I was a freshman, two of my friends and I got tickets to see Buddy play at George Devine's Million Dollar Ballroom on a cold, snowy day. Also on the bill were Ritchie Valens, J.P. "The Big Bopper" Richardson, Dion and the Belmonts, and Buddy's backup band, which included a young Waylon Jennings. It was a sold-out show, and the musicians did not disappoint.

I had brought my autograph book with me just in case, so after the show, my friends and I ran to the back where the bands' buses were parked. When Buddy and the rest exited the stage door, the crowd rushed them. I never did get an autograph, but Valens came by to say hello and shake our hands. The musicians boarded their buses, then flew on to Iowa. The show they played there was their last.

I came home on Feb. 3 and turned on the radio. A news flash announced that a plane carrying Holly, Valens and the Big Bopper had crashed in an Iowa cornfield. All three, plus the pilot, were killed. The only thing I could do was sit at my kitchen table and sob.

A few years later, my Marquette senior prom was held at the ballroom. I was still so distraught over Buddy's death that I couldn't bring myself to attend.

LARRY GIANTOMAS
MISHAWAKA, IN

U.S. pop musician Buddy Holly was 22 years old when he died in 1959.

HOLLY: PICTORIAL PRESS LTD/ALAMY STOCK PHOTO; VALENS: AP/SHUTTERSTOCK

Ritchie Valens was 17 when he was killed in a plane crash with Holly.

DONNA WAS HER NAME

On a sunny October day in 1958, a blonde teenager named Donna Ludwig was cruising Southern California's San Fernando Valley. The top was down on her white Ford convertible as the radio blared KFWB, the main Los Angeles rock station. Suddenly a familiar voice wafted from the car speaker: "I had a girl, Donna was her name."

Ludwig—surprised and shocked—instantly recognized both the singer and the tune. It was the song that her recording-artist boyfriend had sung to her over the phone months earlier. But Richard Valenzuela had never told Ludwig that "Donna" would become his next single.

Del-Fi Records owner Bob Keane dubbed his 17-year-old recording sensation Ritchie Valens in order to reach a wider audience. Valens had scored a minor success with "Come On, Let's Go" before "Donna" took off and peaked at No. 2 on the national Billboard charts. Keane also had Ritchie cut a rocked-up version of an old Mexican wedding song called "La Bamba." That upbeat ditty—the B side to "Donna"—has outlasted Valens' ode to his girlfriend.

On Feb. 3, 1959, Ritchie Valens died in an Iowa plane crash along with singers Buddy Holly and J.P. "The Big Bopper" Richardson.
RANDAL C. HILL · BANDON, OR

WHEN BUDDY PLAYED

Texas teen Judy Yocom enjoyed hometown rocker Buddy Holly's music before he became famous.

ATTENDING LUBBOCK HIGH SCHOOL IN THE mid-1950s was quite an experience. You see, there was a lot of talk about this guy named Buddy Holly who played guitar with his band at the local roller rink on weekends.

One Friday night, my friends and I decided to go check him out. We all heard the rumor that he could play a mean guitar and sing, too. That's all we needed to motivate us!

After skating around awhile, we took a break for intermission and took off our skates. The band members finally came out to set up their equipment on a platform in the middle of the rink. Buddy was on guitar, Joe Mauldin on bass and Jerry Allison was playing the drums. Everyone was unusually quiet, waiting to hear them play.

When the music started, we all danced. I loved it all: the lyrics, the rock 'n' roll, the dancing. Buddy, who graduated two years before me, wasn't good-looking—he was really tall and lanky—but he could rock! I became a fan.

Luckily, Joe, the bassist, lived two blocks from me. Whenever the band practiced in his garage, my girlfriend and I would dance outside in the middle of the street as they played.

A talent scout discovered Buddy in 1955, and our local hero began to make it big. When Buddy died in a plane crash four short years later, the tragic news devastated the whole town. I went to his funeral. At 22 years old, he was just getting his start and beginning to write such beautiful music.

To this day, I love Buddy's music. For my 60th birthday, my sons took me to see the Buddy Holly Show at a theater in Denver. The guy that played Buddy looked just like him with the glasses, and he nailed the Texas accent. I even got up to dance in the aisles—just as I did when I was a teenager!

JUDY YOCOM · AURORA, CO

Lillian (inset) heard the music of Ray Charles one night in 1954 and was hooked.

Experiencing a Music Revolution

Growing up, I listened to my parents' music on Martin Block's *Make Believe Ballroom* radio program. But one night in 1954, I heard a catchy new song being played by disc jockey Alan Freed, aka Moondog, on WINS radio: "I Got a Woman" by Ray Charles. I'd never experienced anything like it before.

When rhythm and blues music like this first aired, many called it "race music," but it soon crossed over to traditionally white radio stations. Oh, yes, the times were changing.

Some of the guys in the Brooklyn housing projects where my family lived formed their own musical groups and gathered to harmonize in the hallway outside our door. Boy, they sounded so good. Among these singers was Frankie Lymon, who formed the Teenagers, an early rock band that later topped charts with "Why Do Fools Fall in Love."

I couldn't get enough of this soulful sound. With my weekly allowance of $1, I bought a new 78 record every week. I soon owned a nice collection that included Bo Diddley, Faye Adams, Fats Domino, the Harptones, Johnny Ace, Clyde McPhatter and the Paragons. Along with all this new music, I wore poodle skirts and bobby socks and learned some new dance moves.

One day, after I got permission from my parents, my friends and I rode the train downtown to attend Alan Freed's rock 'n' roll show at the Brooklyn Paramount Theatre. With policemen out in force to keep order, the line wrapped around the block.

In the packed theater the excitement grew. Red Prysock and the Treniers opened the show, and then Moondog came out to announce the lineup of musicians to follow, including the outrageous Little Richard and Jerry Lee Lewis. The place went wild: The balcony actually shook as we danced in the aisles!

It all came tumbling down for Alan Freed in the late '50s, when he was accused of accepting bribes to play certain records on his radio program. I read about the payola accusation in the newspaper and was disappointed in him, but I never forgot the man who introduced me to rock 'n' roll music.

I'm so glad I grew up in the '50s.

LILLIAN PIETRI • CHARLOTTE, NC

FROM ONE MUSICIAN TO ANOTHER

A bond forms when people speak the same language.

HE WAS A 36-YEAR-OLD veteran recovering from brain surgery in November 1951, lying in a bed at what is now the Zablocki Veterans Affairs Medical Center in Milwaukee, Wisconsin. He had just come out of a postoperative coma, and something wonderful was about to happen. A music lover, he was soon to meet one of his idols, Les Paul.

Paul and his wife, Mary Ford, were at the peak of their popularity at that time and would go on to record hits such as "Mockin' Bird Hill," "How High the Moon" and "Vaya Con Dios." They were rocking the music world with their rare blend of guitar and dubbed-harmony voices. On that day, the two were visiting veterans at the hospital during a trip to Milwaukee. (Paul was from nearby Waukesha, Wisconsin).

The veteran was my dad, Dean Davis. When the couple came to my dad's room to play for him, Daddy cried. He also was a musician and played guitar, mandolin and violin. After his brain surgery, the right side of Daddy's body was paralyzed, and he feared he would never play again. Les, however, assured him that he could learn to play left-handed. Les had been in a car accident and had overcome a bad elbow injury that had threatened his career.

My dad asked to hear a song, and Les played it for him with his left hand. He asked Les to play the song in the key of D flat—difficult to play. Les complied, and a friendship began. They found out that they were close in age (one month apart), and with their shared love of music, the pair clicked.

The plight of this sick veteran touched the hearts of Les and Mary. After they left my dad's room, they decided to have a left-handed guitar made especially for him. Daddy died on Nov. 19, 1951, one day before the guitar arrived.

DAWN DAVIS WESENBERG
WISCONSIN RAPIDS, WI

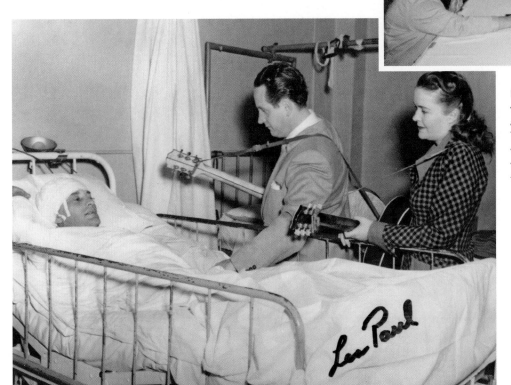

Les Paul, left, and wife Mary Ford play at Dean's bedside. The duo kept in touch with Dawn, above with Paul, and her family for years.

Among the Mourners, a Humble Icon

I n March 1952 the Grand Ole Opry's first superstar, Uncle Dave Macon, died. Uncle Dave had been with the show from the beginning, playing banjo, singing and telling jokes. He was also my grandfather.

At age 81, he sang his last song at the Opry's Ryman Auditorium, sitting in his usual chair during the performance, with his son Dorris strumming guitar at his side. Still on stage, Uncle Dave whispered to Dorris that he was too weak to stand. So Dorris and the stagehands picked up Uncle Dave, chair and all, and carried him off. He died three weeks later.

Uncle Dave's funeral was in his hometown of Murfreesboro, Tennessee, southeast of Nashville. Many stars of the Opry came to pay their respects, including Opry founder "Solemn Ole Judge" George D. Hay.

The church was overflowing with mourners, and many had to wait outside. A tall, lanky man in a cowboy hat showed up, with humble apologies for being late. He told a couple of people that he'd become lost in Murfreesboro and that a police officer had given him directions to the church. The man didn't try to force his way inside; he waited patiently in the churchyard with other mourners for the remainder of the funeral.

Through the years, the Macon family has often wondered if mourners standing near the soft-spoken man ever knew that he was Hank Williams, one of the greatest country music stars of all time. Sadly, Hank himself died less than a year later, on New Year's Day 1953, at age 29.

MARY MACON DOUBLER
FAYETTEVILLE, TN

When Uncle Dave died, Hank Williams (left) came to the funeral.

WILD FOR CASH

While a student at the University of Kansas in the late 1950s, I went to a concert of Grand Ole Opry stars in Topeka. The headliner was a new singer named Johnny Cash. Johnny had released only a few songs at that time. He sang "I Walk the Line," "There You Go" and "Train of Love" during his set and then again for his encore. The crowd went wild, so he sang them again! I really liked his lead guitarist, Luther Perkins, who had a very distinctive style.

PAUL HEITZMAN · EUDORA, KS

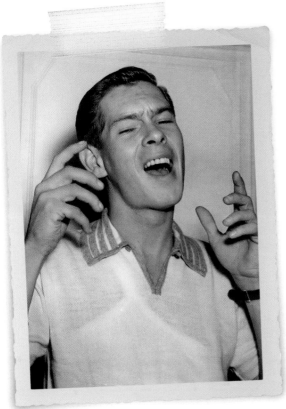

Johnnie Ray was discovered singing at Detroit's legendary Flame Show Bar, a prestigious outlet for headlining black musicians during the 1950s.

AN EMOTIONAL RESCUE

CHURCHILL KOHLMAN WAS AN AFRICAN-AMERICAN night watchman who spent his days writing ballads. His lifelong dream of success materialized late in 1951. That's when a rhythm-and-blues-loving, almost-deaf white singer from Dallas, Oregon, recorded his song "Cry" for Columbia Records.

With this tune, John Alvin "Johnnie" Ray set a new standard for recorded histrionics. Influenced by his friend, R&B artist LaVern Baker ("Tweedle Dee," "Jim Dandy"), Ray belted out "Cry" ("cuh-RYE") in an emotion-packed, near-breathless studio performance that approached the intensity of some R&B artists.

Early in 1952, Ray's single reached No. 1 simultaneously on both the pop (white) charts and R&B (black) charts. But strangely, Columbia never tried to replicate Johnnie's unique "Cry" feat. Although Ray would hit the Top Ten pop lists six more times during the '50s, Columbia never gave him another chance to make further inroads into the world of rhythm and blues he so loved.

A year later, a small-time Memphis record company owner, Sam Phillips, declared that he could make a billion dollars if he could only find "a white man who sang black." Then one afternoon, a shy, greasy-haired truck driver (also an R&B fan) entered Sun Records' cramped office and said he'd like to make a record. That truck driver was none other than Elvis Presley.

RANDAL C. HILL • BANDON, OR

BACK ON TOP

Bill Haley and His Comets recorded the single "Thirteen Women" for Decca Records in 1954. With 30 minutes remaining to record the flip side—a dance number absurdly labeled a fox trot—the first two takes proved unusable, and studio time ran out. Undaunted, producer Milt Gabler combined those attempts to create the master for "Rock Around the Clock." Disc jockeys preferred the "Clock" side, and the song became a minor hit that year before fading quickly.

The following year, though, the song changed American popular music. When Haley's voice thundered through theater speakers behind the credits for the film *Blackboard Jungle*, teens went crazy and often danced in theater aisles. Decca reissued the disc, which quickly locked in the No. 1 chart position for eight weeks.

Fast-forward 18 years to 1973. George Lucas' movie *American Graffiti* opened with "1, 2, 3 o'clock, 4 o'clock, ROCK!" Six months later, Garry Marshall's new TV series, *Happy Days*, premiered with the same opening theme. The anthem generated so much interest that in 1974, it reached the Top 40 singles list—for the third time in two decades.

RANDAL C. HILL • BANDON, OR

THE STARS CAME TO ATLANTIC CITY
As a teenager, it seems, ESTHER BURCH, of Sequim, Washington, posed with every famous or near-famous rock group or singer who passed through the Philadelphia region in the 1950s.

1. "I was staying at the same hotel as Johnnie Ray. When he got out of the pool, I threw him my towel to dry off. The next day, a fan wanted to buy the towel off me. 'Sure,' I said. 'And I washed it too.' 'You washed it?!' she said. The sale did not go through."

2. "During a Vic Damone concert, my friend and I did the hand jive. Vic stopped singing because the audience was watching us and not him. He called us up onstage and had us stand behind him. It was the only way he could get the audience to look at him."

3. "I met Johnny Mathis many times. He was quiet but always very nice."

4. "Here I am with three of the Four Coins. The fourth is taking the photo."

Teenage Dream

She lived a schoolgirl's fantasy—a date with her favorite boy band, the Four Preps.

I was your average starry-eyed teenybopper during the squeaky-clean days of the 1950s, when Elvis still couldn't be shown below the waist. One of the top bands of the day was the Four Preps, a group that combined humor with infectious beats and great harmonies. Their "26 Miles (Santa Catalina)" stayed on the charts for weeks.

I obsessively watched the group on *American Bandstand*. Glen, the baritone, was blond and good-looking. Ed, the bass, was tall and quiet, while Bruce, the lead singer, was always clowning around. But I had a crush on the redhead tenor with freckles, Marv.

In '59, my local radio station in Oklahoma City staged a promotional contest: Win a Date with the Four Preps. The lucky winner would eat dinner with the boys, attend a concert and hang out backstage. I immediately entered—and won!

I was excited, but cautious. I figured the Preps were being paid to have this "date" with me. I imagined they would just ignore me all evening. After all, they were huge stars and had recently appeared in *Gidget*, a popular teen surfer movie.

On the appointed day, my father drove me to meet them and snap some photos before leaving me on my own. I was determined not to be too giggly, but my resolve lasted just five minutes.

First the Preps introduced themselves—as if they had to! They asked me about my life and joked around. They had me in stitches! By the end of dinner, they'd won me over. I had made four new friends and felt silly for thinking they would ever hurt my teenage feelings.

Every summer after that, they welcomed me backstage if they were performing nearby. Eventually, I went away to college. I would hear their songs on the radio, but I soon learned not to brag that I knew them. Nobody believed me!

JANE THOMPSON · GEORGETOWN, TX

Superfan Jane (above) couldn't believe her good luck when she won a date with the Four Preps. The band members joked around with her and helped starstruck Jane (left) feel comfortable in 1959.

During the band's last concert at the Oxford Circle Jewish Community Center, Barry, first row far left, and a few others played out of sync. No one seemed to notice.

Playing in the Band

When I was about 7 or 8, my mother asked me whether I'd like to learn to play a musical instrument. After a few days, I decided on the accordion.

At the time, the accordion was quite a popular instrument—accordionists were featured regularly on TV variety shows throughout the 1950s. Plus, the instrument was big, shiny and complex, with piano keys, buttons and a bellows that worked to move air and make the reeds vibrate.

I took lessons at Mr. Brown's Music School on Castor Avenue in Northeast Philadelphia, Pennsylvania. My teacher was Mr. Black. After a couple of years, so many accordionists joined me that the school figured it could capitalize on this trend by forming an all-accordion band.

We played for civic and religious organizations in the neighborhood for the next year or so until we ran out of gigs. I have no idea if they were paying gigs, but I don't remember receiving any compensation. I just recall playing our hearts out for crowds of noisy adults more engaged in eating and talking with each other than listening to an orchestra featuring nothing but accordions.

I stopped playing the accordion about the time puberty kicked in. Girls didn't seem interested in accordion players. Elvis Presley was wowing them with his guitar, and Jerry Lee Lewis with his piano. When I announced to my mom that I was finished with the instrument, she took it back to Mr. Brown's Music School and traded it in for the acoustic guitar of her dreams.

BARRY KUSHNER
PHILADELPHIA, PA

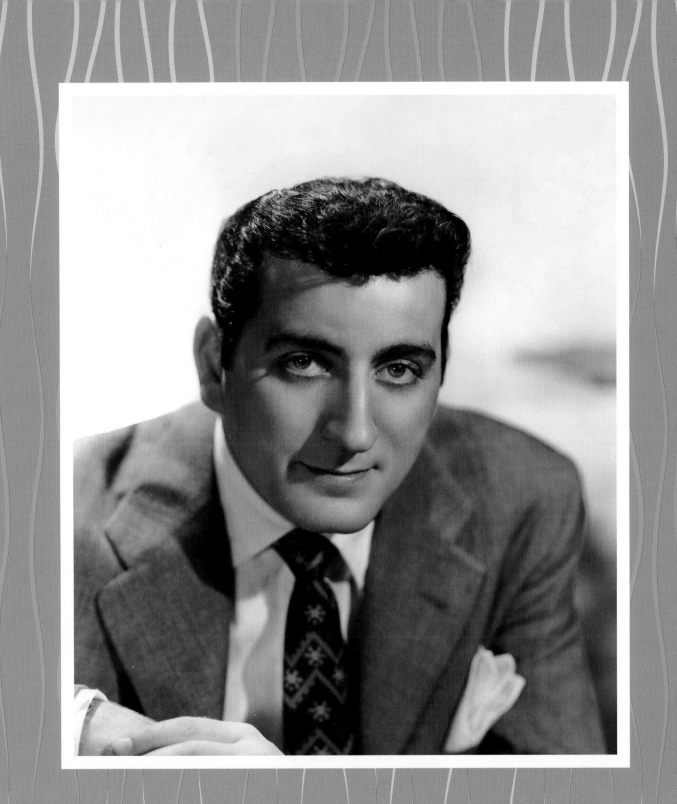

Tony Bennett Was Kind

In 1952, my family visited New York City and Radio City Music Hall. On the bill that night were Patti Page, Bill Hayes and Lola Lee, but the headliner was Tony Bennett. Most girls were screaming and pushing their way to the stage. Not my older sister and I. We were shy girls from Akron, Ohio. Mr. Bennett spotted us in the back and, recognizing that we were not typical New York City girls, motioned for my sister to come up front. He then signed and handed her his script! I've carried this lesson in humility throughout my life.

GRETCHEN FISHER · HOMERVILLE, OH

THE TV SERIES *The Lone Ranger* struck a chord with viewers, running from 1949 to 1957. It starred Clayton Moore as the Lone Ranger, riding Silver, and Jay Silverheels as Tonto, riding Scout.

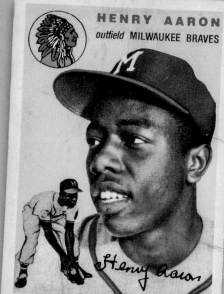

THAT'S ENTERTAINMENT

Stars could really shine with the popularity of TV, movies and the accessibility to sports in the 1950s.

HERE THEY COME

The sitcom launched in 1951, and by January 1955, the *I Love Lucy* cast—Lucille Ball, Vivian Vance, Desi Arnaz and William Frawley—began a cross-country drive in the episode "California, Here We Come!"

LUCY LORE

Within five months of its October 1951 debut, *I Love Lucy* was the top-rated show on TV. Except for the 1955-'56 season (when it was beaten by *The $64,000 Question*), it held on to that spot for the rest of its run.

....

It was the first TV program to be filmed by three moving cameras before a live audience—a system still used today.

....

The show was black-and-white in real life, too—at least a little. Karl Freund, director of photography, had the set for the Ricardos' New York apartment painted in shades of gray because he'd just devised a "flat lighting" system for three moving cameras and he didn't want to have to worry about how colors would translate onto black-and-white TV sets.

....

Lucy and Ricky Ricardo were originally Lucy and Larry Lopez. Those names were changed at the last minute so viewers wouldn't confuse Desi with then-popular bandleader Vincent Lopez.

....

When the cameras weren't rolling, Vivian Vance (Ethel Mertz) and William Frawley (Fred Mertz) didn't care for each other.

....

Saturday-afternoon reruns of *I Love Lucy* placed among the top 10 television shows in 1955, tying with first-run, prime-time episodes of *The Honeymooners*.

Hilarity ensues when Lucy and Ethel try their hand at working in a chocolate factory in "Job Switching."

> *You bought a television set, plugged it in, set up your antenna and shazam! You had every channel in your area—and it was free!*
>
> **KATHLEEN WINDSOR**
> NAUVOO, IL

WHAT'S ON?

IN THE 1950s, HOME ENTERTAINMENT was radically transformed as television turned the dial down on radio. The new medium caught on so fast it was reported that children were spending more hours in front of the tube than in school!

The allure is understandable. *I Love Lucy, The $64,000 Question* and *The Mickey Mouse Club* were irresistibly entertaining.

Variety shows ruled. Americans couldn't get enough of live, vaudeville-inspired programs hosted by the likes of Milton Berle, Ed Sullivan, Jack Benny and George Gobel. ABC, NBC, CBS and the old DuMont network were happy to oblige.

By the end of the decade, girls swooned over TV celebs like Ricky Nelson, young boys idolized Davy Crockett, cowboy wannabes loyally followed *Gunsmoke*, and everybody danced along with Dick Clark's *American Bandstand*.

LEFT: SNAP/REX/SHUTTERSTOCK; RIGHT: MOVIESTORE/SHUTTERSTOCK

GO WEST, YOUNG VIEWER

Although 1957 saw the premiere of two of television's most beloved series, *Leave It to Beaver* and *Perry Mason*, the '57-'58 season is better remembered as the year of the Western. "Horse operas" that debuted that season include *Maverick* and *Wagon Train*, which became viewer favorites. In 1957, eight of the top 20 shows were Westerns, led by *Gunsmoke*, which had premiered in 1955.

26 Men
Arizona Rangers keep the peace.

Boots and Saddles
Adventures of the Fifth Cavalry.

The Californians
A half-hour drama set in San Francisco.

Colt .45
The gun-maker's son is a government spy.

The Gray Ghost
Based on a real Confederate soldier.

Have Gun, Will Travel
A gun-for-hire works out of San Francisco.

Man Without a Gun
A reporter roots out evil in Yellowstone.

Maverick
Gamblers find trouble or it finds them.

The Restless Gun
A Civil War vet roams dangerous territory.

Sugarfoot
An Easterner out west has much to learn.

Tombstone Territory
Battles in the infamous Arizona district.

Trackdown
A Texas Ranger chases bad guys.

Wagon Train
The trials of life on the trail.

Wells Fargo
About an agent for the transport company.

Zorro
The masked avenger saves the day.

THE WAY WEST
The stars of *Wagon Train*—Robert Fuller, John McIntire, Michael Burns, Frank McGrath and Terry Wilson—pose for a promo shot. The popular show about 19th-century migrants was one of 15 TV Westerns that debuted in 1957, along with *Leave It to Beaver*.

"

We loved the neat morals the show [Leave It to Beaver] embraced. At the time, I was dating the man who would become my husband, and we often said that if we had a son, we'd call him Beaver. We did marry, and our 50-something son has been nicknamed "The Beaver" all these years.

GAIL BEAUCHAMP · RED LODGE, MT

RELATING TO THE BEAV

MY FAVORITE FAMILY sitcom when I was growing up was *Leave It to Beaver*. I'd quickly change out of my school clothes and into my playclothes when I got home so I could watch *Leave It to Beaver* before heading outside.

As an adult I see the show as an ideal of the mid-20th-century suburban family. As a child, I enjoyed watching the antics of The Beaver because he reminded me of myself. I seemed to be in similar situations, both at school and at home. Seeing someone else getting into trouble and having to pay the consequences took a bit of the sting out of all the disciplinary actions my mom used on me to reinforce whatever rule she wanted me to follow.

I've seen reruns of all the episodes many times. I'd watch it routinely up to my teenage years. When I got to Johnston Junior High School in Houston, Texas, I became more a fan of *Dark Shadows*, which also ran on weekdays after school, beginning in 1966.

JOANNE CLAYTON
HERRIN, IL

THE HAPPY FAMILY
Ward Cleaver (Hugh Beaumont) and June (Barbara Billingsley) hardly ever shouted at their boys, even when they didn't do what they were told. In my favorite episode, "The Bank Account," Ward wants Wally (Tony Dow) and Beaver (Jerry Mathers) to deposit money into their college savings, but instead they withdraw cash to surprise their dad with a new hunting jacket. Ward is angry before he realizes what they've done. "I guess I jumped to conclusions," he tells them. "I apologize."
ANN HYATT · UNION GROVE, AL

Leave It to Beaver ran from '57 to '63, first on CBS, then on ABC, and in reruns for decades.

SEEING STARS

These celebrities from the silver screen made palms sweat and pulses race.

MARILYN MONROE

If this blond bombshell didn't make a man's heart rate go up, he needed a doctor. Monroe radiated an intoxicating blend of vulnerability and sensuality, combined with impeccable comic timing. Yet behind all that, the star of *Gentlemen Prefer Blondes* and *Some Like It Hot* also exuded a sense of melancholy that foreshadowed her death in 1962.

JAMES DEAN

A smoldering symbol of youthful rebellion, James Dean definitely epitomized teenage cool—a persona he honed in his films. There wasn't a cooler image at the time than Dean in a jean jacket with a cigarette dangling haphazardly from his lips. His bright career, however, was brief. His tragic death in a car accident at the age of 24 only solidified his live-fast, die-young legend.

MARLON BRANDO

Females swooned over this brooding hunk, who stormed to fame with a tour-de-force performance in *A Streetcar Named Desire*. He cemented his status as a superstar with equally mesmerizing roles in *The Wild One* and *On the Waterfront*, for which he won an Academy Award in 1954.

ELIZABETH TAYLOR

This starlet's life was the stuff of Hollywood legend. Taylor achieved supercelebrity status via blockbusters like *Cat on a Hot Tin Roof, Cleopatra, Butterfield 8* and *Who's Afraid of Virginia Woolf?* Eight marriages to celebrities like Eddie Fisher and Richard Burton, combined with a lifestyle as flamboyant as the diamonds she sported, only added luster to her name.

FILM & STAGE FAVORITES

ALL THE WORLD WAS A STAGE IN THE fabulous '50s. Film favorites from the decade include *The Creature from the Black Lagoon, White Christmas, Guys and Dolls, An American in Paris, A Streetcar Named Desire, Love Me Tender, Around the World in 80 Days, The King and I, The 10 Commandments, Invasion of the Body Snatchers, The Bridge on the River Kwai* and *Oklahoma!*.

Younger moviegoers discovered the power of Disney as *Cinderella, Alice in Wonderland, Peter Pan* and *Sleeping Beauty* captured their imaginations.

Jump to the East Coast, and fabulous productions including *South Pacific* and *My Fair Lady* dazzled theater audiences on the Great White Way.

A REBEL WITHOUT PAUSE

On Sept. 30, 1955, James Dean died after his Porsche Spyder crashed into another car. Though he starred in only three films—*Rebel Without a Cause*, *East of Eden*, and *Giant*—decades later, the actor is hard to forget.

A BRUSH WITH THE LEGEND

A carload of us teenagers drove a 1953 Plymouth two-door from Indianapolis to Fairmount, Indiana, to visit James Dean's grave a month after his fatal accident. Chunks of tombstone had already been chipped off by souvenir hunters. Afterward, we drove to the home of Mr. and Mrs. Marcus Winslow—Dean's aunt and uncle who raised him on their farm. Mrs. Winslow invited us in, then brought out a family photo album. One picture was of a young James Dean opening Christmas presents while sitting in a big overstuffed chair. I looked down at the chair I was sitting in, and it was the same one.

DALE MORTENBECK · INDIANAPOLIS, IN

WANTING TO BE JAMES DEAN

I grew up in the early '50s—a time of change and turmoil. Wanting to fit in, my friends and I flocked to the movies to learn how to be rebellious juvenile delinquents. James Dean and Marlon Brando were our role models. The main takeaway was they didn't do what they were told. The obligatory dress code called for black boots with a buckle on the side, a black leather garrison belt and a pair of Levi's worn so low, the seat of the pants bagged out. My parents wouldn't buy the high-priced Levi's. I got Wranglers. It was embarrassing.

BILL ABRAMS · PINE PLAINS, NY

Allan (left) falsified his age and joined the Coast Guard at 14; (above) Leslie Caron, in *An American in Paris.*

RUNAWAY FEAR

Godzilla (1954) was the first movie on the big screen that my cousin and I saw, and boy, was it memorable—but not because of the monster. When Godzilla first appeared, my cousin jumped out of his seat, tossing his popcorn, and ran up the aisle. My dad caught him before he could run out of the theater.

After some coaxing, my cousin returned to his seat and was able to watch the rest of the movie. To this day, Godzilla remains my favorite monster.

BARBARA ADAMCIK · FREEMANSBURG, PA

AN AMERICAN IN (THE SOUTH OF) PARIS

In 1954, when I was in the U.S. Coast Guard, I was assigned to an island in the South Pacific. Bored to tears, I watched the movies *Lili* and *An American in Paris*. I instantly fell in love with the beautiful star of both films, Leslie Caron.

For decades afterward, I followed her career. Cut to 1996, when I heard she'd opened an inn just south of Paris. My wife and I visited and met Ms. Caron. Needless to say, I was a nervous wreck and for a few seconds was actually speechless. I guess I still have a crush on her.

ALLAN STOVER · THE VILLAGES, FL

James, a small-town Wild One, wore a black jacket and rode a Harley, not a Triumph.

JUST LIKE MARLON BRANDO

I grew up in the small town of Manistique, Michigan, which had a population of around 5,000. My childhood hero was Marlon Brando. Back in 1958, when I was 18, I owned a 1949 Harley, one of three motorcycles in town.

In those days, people in town considered me an outlaw because I wore a black jacket and rode my bike. When the movie *The Wild One* came out, all the girls wanted to ride with me. Of course, they couldn't let their parents know that they went for a ride with the hometown Wild One.

I still ride today, as do both my sons. But I'm not called the Wild One anymore.

JAMES STEWART · GRAFTON, WI

FAME

Vintage Ads

The 1950s sure brought on many delightfully entertaining options for the viewing public.

The new Sport Shirt Look in "I LOVE LUCY" PAJAMAS by Harwood

Lucille Ball and Desi Arnaz, TV stars, in "I Love Lucy" Pajamas

FOR CASUAL WEAR around the house, — for restful easy slumber — team up, look elegant in "I Love Lucy" pajamas! You'll enjoy your leisure together more . . . and you won't have to "run for cover" when the doorbell rings!"Coat has smart widespread collar; trousers are cut like tailored slacks — with cuffs and roomy patch pockets! (Gals, discover how adorable you look in men's pajamas!) A gorgeous "double-barreled" gift—for "Her and Him!" Men's Sizes—A, B, C, D. Women's Sizes—AA (10), A (12-14), $6.95 B (16-18), C (20).

At fine stores everywhere or write

Harwood Manufacturing Corp.
261 FIFTH AVENUE • NEW YORK 16, N. Y.

110

1953

DID YOU buy pajamas to match Lucy and Desi's? The his-and-her pj's certainly look comfortable for diehard fans of *I Love Lucy* to lounge around and watch the show.

1952

WITH ITS enormous cast, celebrity cameos (look for Bob Hope and Bing Crosby munching popcorn) and, not least, glorious Gloria Grahame bossing around an elephant, *The Greatest Show on Earth* is everything you want in a Cecil B. DeMille epic—overheated, campy and completely entertaining. It took the Oscar for best picture of 1952, a win some regard as undeserved. But the best reason to see it again is for DeMille's shots of the real circus as it used to be.

Vintage Ads

Movies were fun for the whole family, and what child wouldn't want a View-Master to play director?

1950

FOR ALL THE FAMILY

NEW VIEW-MASTER FULL COLOR PICTURES THAT "COME TO LIFE" IN THREE DIMENSIONS

They're lifelike...instructive...entertaining! Every member of your family will be amazed by the true-to-life beauty, color and depth of View-Master's new stereoscopic picture releases. Subjects include Egypt and Alaska for "armchair travellers"; The Easter Story, Adventures of Tarzan, Performing Elephants for children. Pictures are mounted in durable, easily stored, seven-scene Reels for use in View-Master Stereoscopes and Projectors. Over 400 different Reels now available at selected Photo, Gift, and Department Stores. View-Master Stereoscope $2.00. Non-stereo Jr. Projector $9.95. Reels 35c each, 3 for $1.00. Slightly higher in Canada.

FOR 3 DIMENSION VIEWING
ASK TO SEE

FULL COLOR PICTURES
FOR 2 DIMENSION PROJECTION

VIEW-MASTER TOYS were like mini projectors that kids—or anyone—could use to rotate through movie stills, circus animals and more on circular discs. To see these images in color was all the more exciting in the '50s.

1953

SENSATIONALISM RULED in movie poster design, especially in sci-fi movies of the 1950s. *It Came from Outer Space* was no exception. This poster emphasizes the film was "in 3-Dimension." Wow!

Mitzi Gaynor sings "I'm Gonna Wash That Man Right Out Of My Hair" in *South Pacific*, about love during WWII. The 1958 movie musical was one of the biggest hits of the decade, earning more than $36 million in the U.S.

ONE ENCHANTED EVENING

MOVIES IN MY CHILDHOOD WERE in black-and-white, measuring 12 inches across the screen of our Admiral TV set. Then one day in 1958, I learned I was going to a real theater to see my first real movie, *South Pacific*.

Almost 7, I felt grown-up going with our neighbor, who was 16 and the most sophisticated person I knew. We wore dresses and our Sunday shoes. I took a sweater in case I got cold from the air conditioning, still a novelty then. My father chauffeured us to the State Theater in Columbus, Ohio, and the adventure began. I remember feeling sheer excitement at seeing the vivid colors on the huge screen. The action, music and scenery captivated me, even though I didn't fully understand the World War II setting. Despite my age, I recognized *South Pacific* as a love story between Emile de Becque and Nellie Forbush, one I still enjoy watching.

CINDY VIOLET · DELAWARE, OH

MORE THAN 60 YEARS AGO, *MY FAIR LADY* LIT UP BROADWAY

On March 15, 1956, theatergoers could have danced all night after seeing the Broadway musical *My Fair Lady*. Starring Rex Harrison and Julie Andrews, it told the story of Eliza Doolittle, a poor flower peddler whose rough, Cockney world is turned upside down by wealthy linguist Henry Higgins. Based on George Bernard Shaw's *Pygmalion*, the show ran for 2,717 performances and won the Tony Awards for best musical and best actor.

People wait in line to buy tickets for the Broadway musical *My Fair Lady* at the Mark Hellinger Theatre in New York City in 1956.

1 2 3 4 5 6 7 8 9 10 R H E   AT BAT

BKLYN   0 0 0 0 0 0 0   0 0 0
YANKS   0 0 0 1 0 1 0 0   2 5 0

Don Larsen's perfect game in 1956 was the first ever in a World Series. There hasn't been one since. The Yankees went on to win the series in Game 7, thumping the Dodgers 9-0.

New York Yankees ballplayers celebrate another World Series victory at Ebbets Field in 1956 (above).

Perfect Day for a Perfect Game

Don Larsen's perfect game played out more than 60 years ago. I was a senior at Nutley High School in New Jersey in 1956, and I have fond memories of that glorious October afternoon.

Back then, New York baseball, consisting of the Yankees, Dodgers and Giants, was the very best on the planet. No matter which team you rooted for, you had a strong chance to enjoy bragging rights.

In Game 5 of the 1956 World Series, the New York Yankees were playing their rivals, the Brooklyn Dodgers, at Yankee Stadium. Not only did the Yankees' Don Larsen have a no-hitter going, but he also had a perfect game in the works.

The halls and classrooms of school were abuzz with the news. When classes ended for the day, those of us on the football team headed down to the locker room. As we trickled through the door in twos and threes, we found our coaches, Sandy Phillips, Ed Deitch, Lou Zwirek and Ralph D'Andrea, huddled around the radio.

On any other day, they would have been scurrying about the locker room exhorting players to get into practice uniforms and start running laps. But not that day.

On that day, there was a sense that history was about to be made. And all of us wanted to be a part of it.

It was the top of the ninth inning, with two out. Brooklyn's Dale Mitchell, a .312 lifetime hitter, was batting. Announcer Bob Wolff called the play-by-play: "Larsen is ready, gets the sign—two strikes, one ball. Here comes the pitch. Strike three! A no-hitter, a perfect game for Don Larsen!"

The locker room erupted with cheers and curses. Immediately, the coaches became coaches again, doing what all coaches do, saying: "C'mon, guys, fun's over. Let's get out there, we've got work to do."

We would have to wait until we got home to watch the evening news and see the now-iconic footage of catcher Yogi Berra leaping into Larsen's arms after the Yankees' 2-0 victory. History was indeed made that day.

DICK NEUBERT · NUTLEY, NJ

TOO MANY COKES AT YANKEE STADIUM

MY GRANDFATHER WAS a baseball fanatic and a huge New York Yankees fan. On Oct. 8, 1956, he took my father, my older brother and me to the fifth game of the World Series, pitting the New York Yankees against the Brooklyn Dodgers. Don Larsen was pitching—the Perfect Game, as it turned out. So marked my introduction to major league baseball.

To be honest, I was not a baseball fan. I went because I was forced to go, to make my grandfather happy. My consolation for sitting in the hot sun for a few hours between third base and home plate was all the hot dogs I could eat, plus all the Coke I could drink.

By the end of the third inning I had to go to the bathroom. My dad took me, although he really was not happy about it. By the end of the sixth inning, believe it or not, I had to go again. This time, my father refused to take me and Grandpa would not budge. I was 10, too young to go by myself, so my brother was told to escort me.

On the way back from the bathroom, I bought another Coke from a vendor. In the top of the ninth, when the Dodgers came to bat, I had to make another trip to the restroom. My dad, grandfather and brother ignored my pleas. Apparently, something big was happening. Three more outs, and Larsen would have pitched a perfect game.

"I have to go."
"Hold it."
"But…"
"Hush!"

Three excruciating outs later, my dad and grandfather were too busy cheering Larsen's historic victory to consider my predicament. I was in tears. My brother finally gave in and took me to the bathroom. Dad and Grandpa never missed me.

It's sad to say that despite my being there—50 feet from home plate at the Perfect Game— what I remember most is that I nearly wet my pants.

PATRICK FAGAN
THE VILLAGES, FL

HEY, ROOKIE!

In 1954, I wrote to the Milwaukee Braves and asked if they could send over a player to speak to our club at the University of Wisconsin-Whitewater. Since we didn't have much of a budget, they sent a rookie. He was thin and shy and not a great speaker, but it was fun being around a major leaguer and hearing the stories of how hard he'd worked to get to the big leagues. Needless to say, nobody asked for his autograph, since he was an untested rookie and probably wouldn't be around long anyway. Little did we know what sort of career that rookie, Henry Aaron, would go on to have.
JIM WOLFF
BERLIN, WI

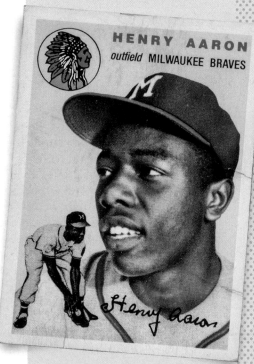

Jack Nicklaus, 13, of Columbus, Ohio, the youngest in a field of 128, won his first-round match of the U.S. National Junior Golf Tournament in Tulsa, Oklahoma, in 1953. His beaming father, L.C. Nicklaus, congratulated the young golfer on his victory.

The Kid

Growing up in Pontiac, Michigan, I was raised to believe "the only good thing in Ohio is the road out of it." That view was soon to be challenged.

In the late 1950s, I worked as a golf caddie at the Buick Open, where I was assigned to an unknown amateur. I can't say I was impressed when we first met. He didn't look much older than me and could have used some fitness training. It was going to be a long week.

Before each round, the players would hit balls off the practice tee. They supplied their own "shag" balls, so the caddies would stand out in the practice range and shag, or retrieve, them, usually 250 yards from the tee. But the kid could really "grip it and rip it," so I stood 75 yards beyond the other caddies, in the weeds. The first day, I lost a third of his shag balls. He would

have to adjust how many balls he could hit/lose per day. On Sunday, we skipped the practice range altogether. No balls; I'd lost them all.

The course was new to me, so I wasn't familiar with the distances, the hazards or the greens, which meant I couldn't advise him on anything. I must have been the worst caddie he'd ever had. And yet the kid never uttered a disparaging word.

But he could chip and putt with the best of them, and as a result, he ended up in 12th place—great for an amateur. Afterward, I met his family, all as gracious and humble as he. They thanked me, and we parted. And yes, he paid well.

It was then that I realized there was one more good thing to come out of Ohio. The kid from Columbus: Jack Nicklaus.

JOE HEITJAN · BENZONIA, MI

Davy in Training

My brother Bob McDonald sure was a cutie at 2, seen here wearing a tot-size Davy Crockett outfit. He was standing outside our family home in Loretto, Pennsylvania. It was 1955, and *Davy Crockett*, a five-part serial starring Fess Parker, was airing on ABC as part of the *Disneyland* series.
GENEVIEVE CATINA · DUNCANSVILLE, PA

HAVING FUN, the adults clearly seem excited to play with the Erector set that this young boy, dressed in a cowboy outfit, received for Christmas in 1954.

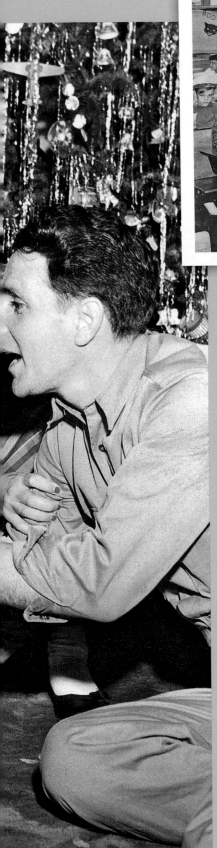

HOLIDAYS AND CELEBRATIONS

Special occasions present plenty of reasons to go all out, making these events even more memorable.

SPECIAL DELIVERY

My cousin David and I sat for this picture in 1954 at our grandmother's house in Clifton, West Virginia. It was my first Easter, and as you can guess from my present, my dad was a taxidermist—a good one, I might add.

KATHY DALTON · RUTLAND, OH

"

Check out the white hats, gloves and purses my sister and I sported on Easter Sunday 1959. When we were old enough, Mom let us pick out our own outfits and ditch the matching dresses we had worn as girls.

JUDY LECLAIRE · ATTLEBORO, MA

MOM MADE A BEAUTIFUL HOLIDAY

My mother was one of the most creative people I've ever known. She cooked, sewed, canned foods from the garden and decorated the house for every season. Each spring, Mom took the Easter hats, headbands and dresses from the previous year to "make them new." She bought new flowers, ribbons and lace, and stayed up late at night finishing her creations. I remember getting up on Easter morning to see our outfits ready for us to put on and wear to church. We always felt so proud to wear what she had made for us. Dad invariably smiled and told us how pretty we looked. Even our little brother, Jim, was sharply dressed! In the photo at right, we are sitting in the bay window of our home, overlooking the Mississippi River in Rice, Minnesota. We had found our hidden Easter baskets and were ready to go to church.

KATHLEEN R. SURMA · ST. CLOUD, MN

From left, Karen, Kathy, Jayne, Peggy and Jim show off their Easter outfits in 1959.

WITH ALL THE FRILLS UPON IT

Sporting rounded cat's-eye frames in 1955, **FLORENCE HOUSEMAN** shows off her homemade Easter bonnet at a family gathering at Fairmount Park in Philadelphia, Pennsylvania. Florence's daughter-in-law **JOAN**, of Philadelphia, says the women in the family would try to outdo one another with their outrageous hats.

PEDALING PATRIOTS

TOM KENNEY of Caldwell, Idaho, sent the photo at left, taken on July 4, 1952, in Steilacoom, Washington, between Tacoma and Olympia on Puget Sound. "The kids were all involved in the organization of the parade," Tom writes. "I'm the one on the left in the foreground, the proud owner of a shiny new Schwinn Black Phantom."

THE RIDE OF HER LIFE

In 1959, I was in sixth grade in Lexington, Massachusetts. My neighbor let me ride his horse in a parade through downtown on Patriot's Day, which celebrates the first battle against the British in the American Revolution.

The kids who owned horses decorated them with red, white and blue crepe paper. My ride was a former racehorse and very high-strung. She was not happy with the crepe paper on her or the other horses. It made her nervous.

We inched along the route in front of the engines from the local fire stations. Suddenly the sirens sounded, and my horse bolted. She galloped the 2 miles right home to the barn, with me hanging on for dear life. We left a trail of red, white and blue crepe paper that I was picking out of the bushes and grass for many months afterward.

SUZY HOPKINS · DENVER, CO

DECORATION DAY

In 1956, my first year as a Boy Scout in West Homestead, Pennsylvania, I marched in my first parade, which commemorated Decoration Day, the forerunner to Memorial Day. The parade ended in a solemn gathering at a cemetery on a hilltop in Munhall, a company town outside of Pittsburgh.

Though World War II had ended 11 years earlier, it remained a painful memory for the people at the cemetery that day. Many had lost someone in the war. My friend Bobby sang "My Buddy," which is about the loss of a close friend. When he finished, the crowd stood silent. Many were sobbing—even the steelworkers had broken down in tears.

Growing up during those early postwar years meant learning about war in terms of heroism and patriotism. It took that Decoration Day parade and ceremony for me to fully understand war's true cost.

GEORGE TOTH · GAITHERSBURG, MD

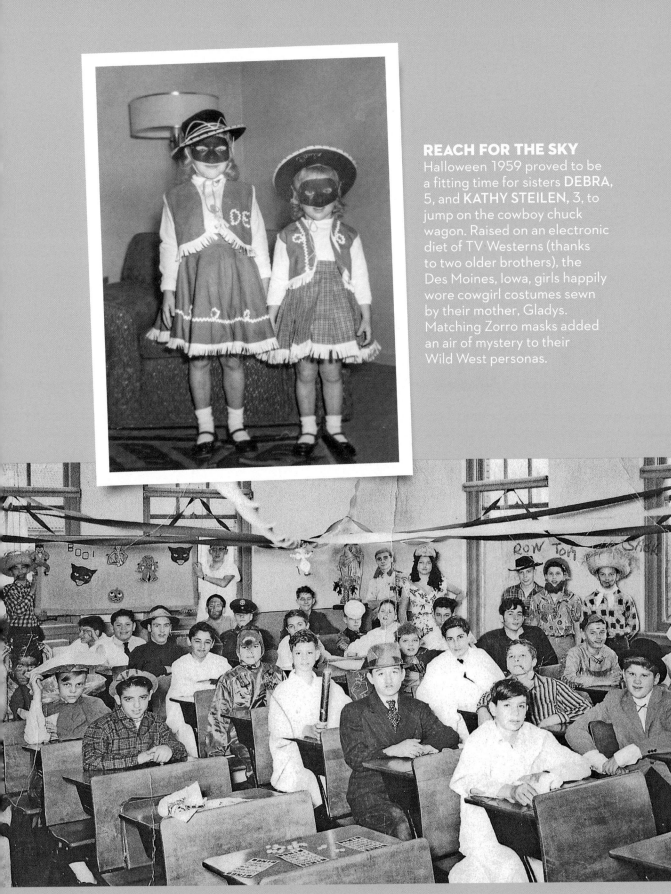

REACH FOR THE SKY

Halloween 1959 proved to be a fitting time for sisters **DEBRA**, 5, and **KATHY STEILEN**, 3, to jump on the cowboy chuck wagon. Raised on an electronic diet of TV Westerns (thanks to two older brothers), the Des Moines, Iowa, girls happily wore cowgirl costumes sewn by their mother, Gladys. Matching Zorro masks added an air of mystery to their Wild West personas.

CLASSY DRESS

Monsignor Campbell threw us a Halloween party in 1958 at Our Lady of Lourdes School in Chicago, Illinois. This was the eighth-grade boys class. I'm at the front of the left-side row.
BRUCE BRAY · KINGSFORD, MI

These salt and pepper shakers have graced our Thanksgiving table since the 1950s. Our grandchildren love to see them every year

ELLEN SCOTT · NAPLES, FL

MOUNT SNOW
"A Thanksgiving Day snowstorm—probably the big one in 1956—left snow piled so high it dwarfed our Chevrolet," says **LOUELLA KIGHTLINGER** of Erie, Pennsylvania.

DOLLED UP
Her eyes closed to the bright sun and her hands protected in a gigantic muff, **PAULA MOHR** braves the brisk weather to pose next to the family's Chevy on Thanksgiving Day in Millington, Michigan, in 1958. Paula's mother, **BARBARA**, snapped the photo.

REFRESHING
Vintage Ads

All holidays call for refreshments, whether a vacation at the beach or a Christmas pit stop for Santa.

HERE'S TO THE JOY OF GLOWING HEALTH!

Florida's vitamin-rich Grapefruit Juice helps fortify you against colds and fatigue 24 hours a day!

A FLORIDA PRODUCT

FLORIDA GRAPEFRUIT JUICE OFFERS ALL THIS HELP TO HEALTH EACH DAY!

1. Helps maintain ALKALINE reserve
2. Supplies LIQUID— hostile to colds
3. A gold mine of VITAMIN C
4. Other VITAMINS and MINERALS
5. ENERGY from fruit sugars
6. Arouses sulky APPETITES
7. Stimulates DIGESTIVE juices
8. MILDLY LAXATIVE

FLORIDA GRAPEFRUIT JUICE IS FULL-STRENGTH — BRIMFUL OF NATURAL HEALTH BENEFITS FOR YOU. NOTHING TO DO BUT HELP YOURSELF!

FLORIDA CITRUS COMMISSION • LAKELAND, FLORIDA

FLORIDA CANNED GRAPEFRUIT JUICE

1950

HOW DOES grapefruit juice compete with beer and soft drinks as a summer beverage? By being the "healthy" choice. Among the beneficial qualities listed are that it "stimulates digestive juices" and is "mildly laxative." Hmm.

It's the little "extras" that make Schlitz the best-liked beer in history

That extra purity born of choice ingredients

That extra delicacy of flavor that delights the true beer lover

That extra smoothness

If you like beer...you'll love Schlitz

Schlitz

The beer that made Milwaukee famous

1952

PRINT ADS for Schlitz beer often featured more than one slogan. Here, the '50s-era saying "If you like beer…you'll love Schlitz" overwhelms the company's longtime slogan at the bottom of the ad, "The beer that made Milwaukee famous." In the 1960s, Schlitz's sales campaign took off with a catchy phrase dreamed up by the ad mavens at Leo Burnett Co.: "When you're out of Schlitz, you're out of beer."

1954

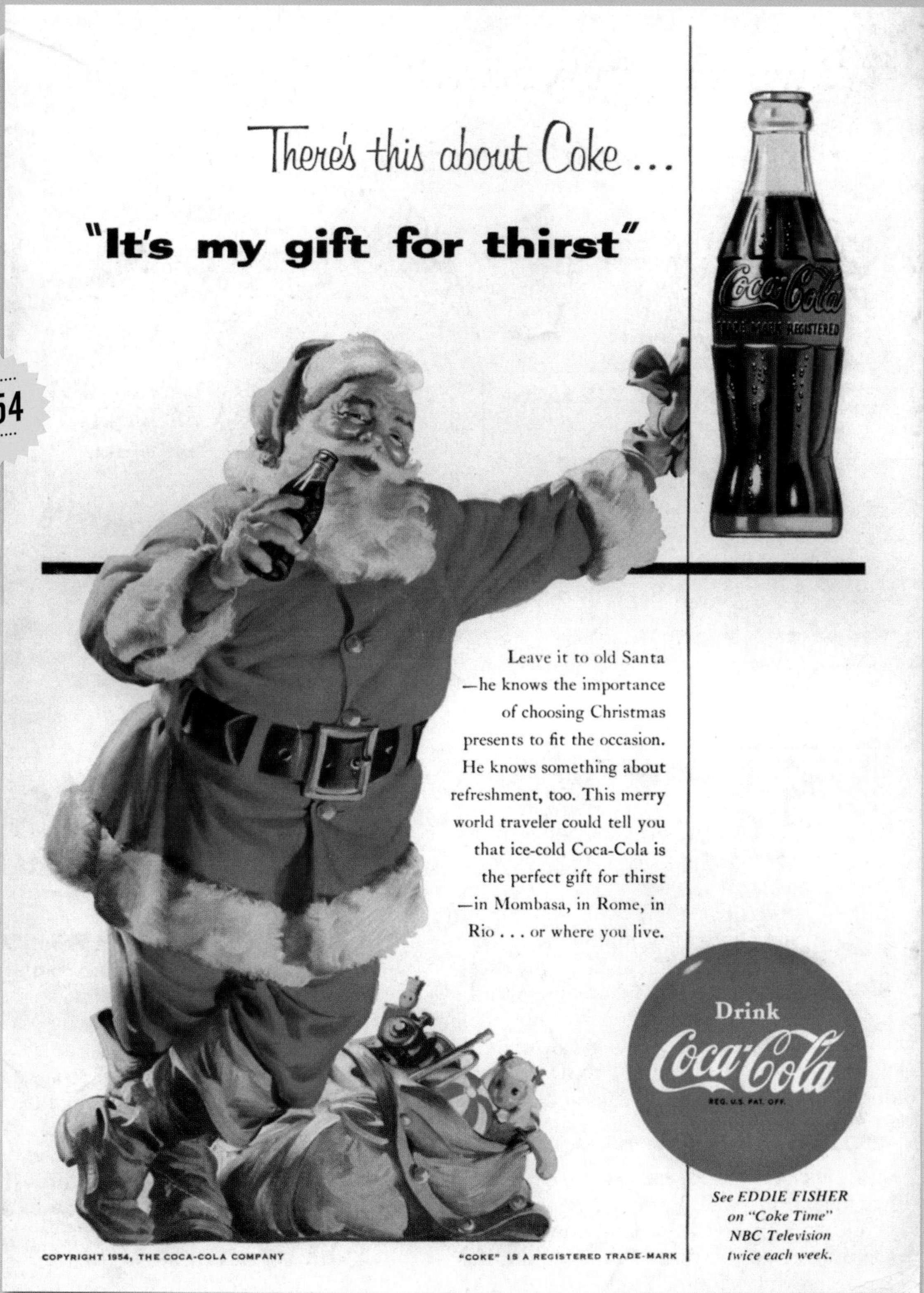
There's this about Coke . . .
"It's my gift for thirst"
Coca-Cola
TRADE MARK REGISTERED
Leave it to old Santa —he knows the importance of choosing Christmas presents to fit the occasion. He knows something about refreshment, too. This merry world traveler could tell you that ice-cold Coca-Cola is the perfect gift for thirst —in Mombasa, in Rome, in Rio . . . or where you live.
Drink
Coca-Cola
REG. U.S. PAT. OFF.
See EDDIE FISHER on "Coke Time" NBC Television twice each week.
COPYRIGHT 1954, THE COCA-COLA COMPANY
"COKE" IS A REGISTERED TRADE-MARK

SANTA LOOKS pretty relaxed taking a break with a Coca-Cola in this holiday ad that hints at the product's international appeal. Also of note here is *Coke Time*, an American musical variety television series that marketed the drink in the '50s, starring Eddie Fisher.

Similar to Fay, these girls delight in the magic of Christmas as they joyfully display their gifts.

'Twas the Night Before

Christmas Eve stirred with excitement.

Christmas Eve 1957, I was 10 and trying to sit still on my grandmother's green mohair couch. The back of my dress was scrunched up behind me and the rough upholstery scratched my bare legs. My older sister, Jane, and younger brother, John, needed no reminders to sit still and wait for dinner. I hated that divan, as my mother called it.

My Aunt Betty and Uncle Bill, who lived next door, were there with their four children, Billy Jo, Timmy, Dick and little sister Terry. We lived just down the hill and we were very close to our cousins.

Grandma Ennis was one of my favorites. At 5 feet 6 inches, with snow white hair, she was always easy to find. That night she wore a lovely apron with a Christmas motif she had designed herself. She made this holiday perfect, and we waited for it all year.

A 4-foot Christmas tree adorned with handblown glass ornaments, bubble lights and tinsel sat on Grandma's TV. Grandma liked to decorate it herself to surprise us when we arrived. Every year the tree had the same decorations, but we always acted surprised.

Brightly colored packages were stacked under the tree, some leaning against the TV cabinet, others spilling onto the living room floor. The boxes and bags were Grandma's works of art. Ribbons matching the wrapping paper wound around each box as if it was the most important gift she was giving. The Christmas stockings she'd made for each of us hung next to the tree.

Before dinner, Grandma would ask Uncle Bill to play Christmas music. The voices of Bing Crosby, Bob Hope and my favorite, Perry Como, drifted around the room, adding to the festivities. Everyone knew the songs by heart: "White Christmas," "God Rest Ye Merry, Gentlemen" and "Rudolph, the Red-Nosed Reindeer." We all sang along and nobody cared if you couldn't carry a tune. This was a family tradition.

My mother, Percy, and Aunt Betty set the table with the good linens and china. They lit candles and heaped food into serving bowls. When dinner was finally served, we each chose a seat around the big cherrywood Windsor table. It was a tight fit, but no one ever suggested that any of us eat at another table.

That year was one of my favorites because my dad, Louis, came home in time to have dinner with us. He worked at the Minneapolis train depot and didn't get holiday pay unless he worked. This year, his boss must have let the men off early.

The food tasted more delicious than ever. This was one of the few times I saw my grandma sit. We laughed and talked about what we wanted for Christmas and discussed the letters we had sent Santa.

After dinner, the women cleared the table, did the dishes and tidied the kitchen. None of the children helped because the kitchen was so small. We were told to wait quietly while they finished.

When the cleanup was done, everyone scrambled to find a place to sit in the living room. Then Grandma handed out the presents, giving each of us children three very similar-looking packages.

We tore open the boxes to find that Grandma had made pajama bags for us with matching pajamas inside. Each bag was a different design—a dog, a cat, a clown. Mine was a pig with ears and a round snout made out of soft pink velvet. With the pj's out of their bags, Grandma showed us how to fold them so they fit back inside and, then, how to use the bags as pillows.

In the next box were crocheted slippers to match our pajamas, and in the last big box,

a bathrobe. I couldn't wait to go to bed that night wearing the cozy bedclothes Grandma had made for me.

The gifts were the best I could have hoped for. The whole night felt special. About 11:30, we left for midnight Mass at St. Therese Catholic Church, a couple of miles away.

Grandma did not join us for the Christmas Eve service and was probably glad to have peace and quiet in her home again. I have no doubt that she cleaned up the mess, stored the dishes in the living room buffet and, before retiring, was making plans for next Christmas Eve.

I loved being up so late and taking part in all of the magic of midnight Mass. The choir sang my favorite carols, the priest told us this was a new beginning, and the smell of incense made it feel that much more important.

When the doors to the church opened and we walked outside, it was snowing lightly. Not enough to be a problem for the cars in the parking lot, but just enough to see Santa's sleigh marks in the snow.

FAY LaVIGNE • MINNETONKA, MN

MEET DR. SEUSS

How the Grinch Stole Christmas!, written and illustrated in 1957 by Dr. Seuss, aka Theodor Seuss Geisel, is a holiday staple. For the TV adaptation of the best-selling children's book, Seuss also wrote the lyrics to all of the songs.

VINTAGE TREASURE

This bright aluminum tree decorated with black bulbs and Buddy Holly-inspired photos and eyeglass frames livens up a shelf in **MARY LYVERS CHISM**'s Pensacola, Florida, home.

A HOLIDAY BEDTIME STORY
My father, Paul Prough Sr., took this photo of me reading from *The Santa Claus Book*, surrounded by my other Christmas gifts (including a Gilbert Erector set), in 1957. To the left, you can see a bit of the model train display Dad always built under our tree.
PAUL PROUGH JR. · MOUNT UNION, PA

"

In the photo below, I was 6 and my brother Dave (on right) was 5 in 1953 when we went to see Santa at the Stone & Thomas department store in Wheeling. It was our Macy's.

JIM FIORILLI • WHEELING, WV

Dec 1957

A PJ CHRISTMAS
On Christmas morning in 1957, the entire **CHAPMAN FAMILY** of Newark, Ohio—Gary, Donna, Rod and baby Chris—dressed in new pajamas, even Donna's doll. Their parents, Don and Dorothy, not pictured here, had a matching set of pj's, too.

FOR THE RECORD

Before one Christmas in the late '50s, I kept hounding my parents for a reel-to-reel tape recorder about the size of a Kleenex box. They didn't have the money for things like that, so imagine my surprise when I saw a Kleenex-size box wrapped under our tree. While nobody was around, I carefully opened it. I couldn't believe it: There was my recorder. I pulled it from the box to check it out. Once satisfied with its quality, I rewrapped it and put it back under the tree.

Come Christmas Day, I unwrapped my present again, jumping for joy and thanking my oblivious parents. Then I hit the Play button.

"Hello," my own voice greeted the room, loud and clear on tape. "This is Robert. This is only a test."

Santa could probably hear the laughter all the way at the North Pole.

ROBERT MORGAN
EL LAGO, TX

LIT WITH LOVE

By mid-December in the late '50s, block after block of our Chicago community was ablaze with Christmas decorations, and just about every house had a glowing tree in its picture window. On frosty nights before Christmas, my family squeezed into the car for our annual ritual of looking at the lights. As Dad navigated through the slippery streets, we'd gasp at the sparkling wonderland that each house staged for our oohs and aahs. We saw Santas and snowmen; lollipops and candy canes; tender scenes of the baby in the manger; and trillions of multicolored lights shining through a blanket of snow. But at the end of the tour, we always agreed: Our own front yard was the most dazzling, most welcoming and most Christmasy of all.

KAREN WERNECKE
HOFFMAN ESTATES, IL

The handknit Christmas stockings, shown here, include two on the top that Frances made for herself and her husband, Charles.

BIG STOCKING, MORE STUFF

Oversize Christmas stockings were a labor of love for avid knitters.

IN THE 1950s, MY MOTHER STARTED A TRADITION by knitting a Christmas stocking for each of my four children. The stockings were quite large and, much to the children's delight, held oodles of goodies. On each was the child's name and birth year. One year my youngest daughter sneaked into the living room, took everything out of her stocking, and then stuffed it all back before she woke us up.

When my mother could no longer knit, I started making stockings for new family members. I'm 98 and still knit simple things, but now, as the family continues to grow, my oldest daughter has taken over the joyful tradition of making the Christmas stockings.

The stockings have become so meaningful that we make sure we bring them when we spend Christmas at another family member's house. A while back, our children came to spend Christmas in Rhode Island with my husband and me. Two days before Christmas, our youngest daughter realized she had forgotten to pack her stocking. Immediately, she called her friend who was house-sitting and had her send the stocking to Rhode Island via overnight mail.

Our family is now scattered around the country, but we still send wrapped stocking stuffers. The children quickly learn that the wrapped gifts in their stockings are not from Santa; they are from family members.

Each year, we look forward to discovering what everyone has sent to stuff in our stockings.

FRANCES B. WOOD · BOSTON, VA

It Takes a Village to Raise a Child's Bike

A last-minute elbow injury is no match for a dad armed with determination.

Johnny and I, along with our two young sons, Barry and Doyle, lived in a small rural community in southern Alabama in 1959. We had bought Barry a bicycle and Doyle a tricycle for Christmas, and had hidden them in the carport, where Johnny would assemble them on Christmas Eve after the kids were asleep.

But on Christmas Eve day, Johnny had to go to Brookley Air Force Base in Mobile, an hour away, to repair a Thunderbird F-100 Super Sabre jet. I had my hands full with baking, preparing for Christmas dinner and caring for two energetic boys.

Just as I was making my favorite frosting for the chocolate cake, a neighbor knocked on the door. Beatrice was the only person on our road with a telephone. The base had called to say that a heavy torque wrench had come apart in Johnny's hand, knocking his elbow out of joint and chipping the bone. My sister-in-law Ruth and her husband, Otto, took me to the hospital while my mother-in-law stayed with the children.

We got there to find Johnny with a cast on his arm, raring to get home despite the doctor's orders that he stay. It was Christmas Eve, Johnny argued, and he had bikes to assemble for his boys. The doctor said he'd consider dismissing him the next morning if Johnny could find someone to drive him home.

On Christmas morning, Johnny contacted the base and was told everyone was off duty; there was no one to drive him home. Then he tried the motor pool. They said orders would have to come from higher up, so Johnny kept making calls. At last, a big blue car with the Air Force insignia rolled up to the hospital asking for the man who needed a lift home so he could put together Christmas bikes for his boys.

Johnny's mother and I were putting dinner on the table when we heard the car. We were thrilled to see Johnny, his arm in a sling, getting out, assisted by a uniformed Air Force officer.

With Otto's help, Johnny assembled the boys' gifts, and they all had a jolly time playing together that afternoon.

Johnny would later require two surgeries on his arm, but those were in the future. That cold Christmas Day, our hearts were full of gratitude for the many people who had gone the extra mile to bring us together on the holiday.

JEANETTE DYESS RYAN
ROBERTSDALE, AL

Barry and Doyle smile with pride atop their newly assembled Christmas gifts.